Freelancing for Television and Radio

Freelancing for Television and Radio is an indispensable guide for those either considering becoming or currently working as a freelance media professional. It offers brief overviews of the TV and radio industries, as well as the role of convergence in video production and multimedia.

Freelancing for Television and Radio explains what it means to be a freelance in the world of the audio-visual industries. From an outline of tax and employment issues it goes on to describe the ups and downs of the world in which the freelance works. Radio, television and related sectors like facilities and video production are assessed for the opportunities they offer the aspiring freelance and there's also an analysis of the skills you need for a successful freelance career. *Freelancing for Television and Radio* includes:

- practical advice on how to make a start; where to find work, writing the right kind of CV, networking and making contacts.

- an important section on maintaining and developing a freelance career as well as a chapter on the challenges and responsibilities of setting up and running a small business.

- a significant chapter on the basics of writing and submitting programme proposals to broadcasters as well as a substantial section of useful contact information.

Leslie Mitchell is a teaching fellow in the Department of Film & Media Studies at the University of Stirling. He has spent most of his career in various kinds of broadcasting from local and network radio, to regional and network television. He has worked on staff, as a freelance and as an independent producer.

Media Skills

SERIES EDITOR: RICHARD KEEBLE, LINCOLN UNIVERSITY
SERIES ADVISERS: WYNFORD HICKS and JENNY McKAY

The *Media Skills* series provides a concise and thorough introduction to a rapidly changing media landscape. Each book is written by media and journalism lecturers or experienced professionals and is a key resource for a particular industry. Offering helpful advice and information and using practical examples from print, broadcast and digital media, as well as discussing ethical and regulatory issues, *Media Skills* books are essential guides for students and media professionals.

English for Journalists, 2nd edition
Wynford Hicks

Writing for Journalists
Wynford Hicks with Sally Adams and Harriett Gilbert

Interviewing for Radio
Jim Beaman

Web Production for Writers and Journalists, 2nd edition
Jason Whittaker

Ethics for Journalists
Richard Keeble

Scriptwriting for the Screen
Charlie Moritz

Interviewing for Journalists
Sally Adams, with an introduction and additional material by Wynford Hicks

Researching for Television and Radio
Adèle Emm

Reporting for Journalists
Chris Frost

Subediting for Journalists
Wynford Hicks and Tim Holmes

Designing for Newspapers and Magazines
Chris Frost

Writing for Broadcast Journalists
Rick Thompson

Find more details of current *Media Skills* books and forthcoming titles at
www.producing.routledge.com

Freelancing for Television and Radio

Leslie Mitchell

Routledge
Taylor & Francis Group

LONDON AND NEW YORK

First published 2005
by Routledge
2 Park Square, Milton Park, Abingdon, Oxon OX14 4RN

Simultaneously published in the USA and Canada
by Routledge
270 Madison Ave, New York, NY 10016

Routledge is an imprint of the Taylor & Francis Group

© 2005 Leslie Mitchell

Typeset in Garamond by Wearset Ltd, Boldon, Tyne and Wear
Printed and bound in Great Britain by MPG Books Ltd, Bodmin

Every effort has been made to ensure that the advice and information in this book is true and
accurate at the time of going to press. However, neither the publisher nor the authors can accept
any legal responsibility or liability for any errors or omissions that may be made. In the case of
drug administration, any medical procedure or the use of technical equipment mentioned within
this book, you are strongly advised to consult the manufacturer's guidelines.

British Library Cataloguing in Publication Data
A catalogue record for this book is available from the British Library

Library of Congress Cataloging in Publication Data
Mitchell, Leslie Scott, 1945–
    Freelancing for television and radio / Leslie Mitchell.—2nd ed.
        p. cm.—(Media skills)
    Includes index.
    1. Broadcasting—Vocational guidance. 2. Broadcasting—Vocational guidance—Great Britain.
    3. Self-employed. I. Title: Freelancing for television and radio. II. Title. III. Series.
    PN1990.55.M58 2005
    791.4402'93—dc22

                                                                                    2004021901

ISBN 0-415-34102-7 (pbk)
ISBN 0-415-34101-9 (hbk)

Contents

Introduction

Throughout my working life I've been aware of freelances. I've worked with freelances and I've been a freelance myself. Most of my career has been spent in the audio-visual industry; in local and network radio, regional and national television, as well as a stint in non-broadcast, corporate work. But I never realised how hard it was to define precisely what a freelance was. Nor had I really thought about the huge range of things you need to know when you're a freelance – and that's not even considering the special skills you need just to do the job. And the job might be a costume designer, sound recordist, camera operator or director or virtually a hundred-and-one other occupations.

Now, year after year, I enjoy teaching students, some of whom, after graduation, go on to work in the audio-visual industries. Some former students have already been stunningly successful; more so than I ever was. Some have received glittering accolades, others in their own quiet way help to form the backbone of this vast, important (and often self-important) business. Every day, they and their colleagues do some of the hundreds of thousands of tasks that have to be accomplished to keep radio, television and non-broadcast communication going. In the course of preparing this book I've had to revisit subjects and ideas that in one way or another I've been familiar with for many years. There has been a great deal of material to read. In addition I've enjoyed many conversations with freelances and those who work with them and those who employ them. This research has reminded me time and again just how massive, sprawling, complicated and unwieldy the audio-visual industry is. It covers a range of skills, aptitudes and creativity which is awe-inspiring and very exciting. For the newcomer to the industry this complexity might seem nearly as daunting and bewildering as it is exciting and attractive.

If you are such a newcomer, or are thinking about a freelance career in the broadcasting or related area, this book has been written with you in mind. There are other publications which deal with careers and work in the audio-visual industry, but here we are concerned particularly with the freelance. This book is an attempt to help you to make your way into a very competitive industry. Once you're there, you may need a guide in order to find your way around. I've tried to draw a map. The purpose of this map is to help you to avoid getting lost. Like all good maps, I've tried to give as much information as I can to help on your way.

Despite the difficulties there are in defining precisely what a freelance is, one thing is certain. Like any other worker, as a freelance you have to have an excellent grasp of the particular skill or craft you're paid to perform. Unlike other workers, in addition to these skills, you have to have an array of other aptitudes too. These include an ability to organise and market yourself and your skills to others, and to control and direct your career. Beside all this, you require a number of business skills too, as well as an inkling about some important legal and tax matters. So, skilled media practitioner, human resources expert, marketer, advertising executive and business person! In a nutshell, that's a freelance.

This book is an attempt to cover the main issues that will confront you as a freelance. It starts with an attempt to work out just what a freelance is, and that's not quite as easy as it sounds! We then go on to look at ways of starting a career and breaking into the business. Maintaining your work as a freelance and developing a strategy for the future occupies us in Chapter 3. Then we move on to look at the specifics of the radio, television and non-broadcast sectors. Developing ideas for programmes is an issue which is a constant preoccupation for many freelances and Chapter 7 gives some guidance on formulating proposals as well as safeguarding your intellectual property. One of the contentions of this book is that all freelances run a business in one form or another, sometimes very humble, sometimes quite grand. Chapter 8 attempts a summary of the areas you will deal with as you run your business. Pressures and ethical dilemmas of various kinds are the subject matter of Chapter 9, which then concludes with a survey of equal opportunity concerns. In the final chapter I've tried to provide the basic information you will need in order to investigate more fully the subject matter of each chapter.

Some of the subjects in this book are complex and at times touch on the law, on tax and on business matters. I am not a lawyer, nor am I a tax or business expert. These areas are touched on because you need to be aware of them; they will affect you in your daily life as a freelance. You should read the relevant chapters, indeed the whole book as an indication, a guide and if appropriate, a warning. There may well be points of law that are relevant to you – the aim of the book is to encourage you to be aware of this and to consult a professional, in this case a lawyer or solicitor. Questions about tax and your obligations to pay it in its many guises will no doubt arise. The advice again is that you should consult a professional; your inspector of taxes, a qualified accountant or quite possibly both. Finally, you shouldn't make financial arrangements without having sound legal and financial advice.

You should seek professional advice on all these matters. However obvious this may seem, many do not do so, and they often regret it. Picking up the pieces if things go wrong takes time and emotional energy. The successful freelance doesn't have an excess of either!

You will have noticed that in this introduction I have talked about freelances. I have not used the term *freelancer*. *Freelance* seems to be the preferred industry expression and it's one which I shall continue to use. In any case, as well as seeming slightly cumbersome, the word *freelancer* now seems to be more closely associated with the hero of a popular computer game. There are a number of other issues of usage which I should clarify. The title of this book refers to *radio and television*, in conversation we tend to refer to *the media*, but this rather general term includes print journalism which is of course beyond the scope of this book. In the official world of statistics, the Department for Education and Skills and the Department of Trade and Industry, we are the *audio-visual industries*.

More importantly, the audio-visual industries are what Skillset is concerned with. At this point I should acknowledge my debt to the work of this organisation and the information it provides. Funded jointly by the industry and government, Skillset is concerned with people and skills for the audio-visual sector. It carries out research and consultation and offers career advice, funding and information in many of the areas which are of crucial concern to the freelance. Much, if not most, of the information about the shape and size of the sector and its workforce comes from Skillset. I have made extensive use of this material, and especially of course the freelance surveys. This information is obtained by distributing questionnaires to freelances through companies within the industry which responded to Skillset's industry census. In fairness I should point out that Skillset urges a degree of caution in the use of this data which, for example, excludes people not working at the time of the survey. Nevertheless in forming a picture of the role of freelances in the audio-visual industries, the survey results are invaluable. I should also acknowledge that although the data is provided by Skillset, the comments (and the responsibility for them), unless specifically attributed, are mine. The relevant reports and a discussion of methodology are freely available on the Skillset website. In any event I would recommend a visit to the site to anyone considering a freelance career in the industry for the wealth of help and information it provides.

There are a number of other usages I should clarify at the outset. We have already considered the audio-visual industry. This comprises a number of *sectors*. Television is a sector, for example, and so of course is radio. Although film is a sector of the audio-visual industry, because of its own distinct practices and particular ways of working it has not been included here. Other terms are a little more difficult to pin down, not least the very word *freelance*, as we shall see in Chapter 1.

Sometimes the words *creative* and *technical* are used almost as opposites, to distinguish, say, a director in the former category, and a camera operator or editor in the latter. I try to avoid this usage. There are many camera operators, editors and lighting experts who are just as creative, if not more so, than those who are sometimes referred to as creatives, a favourite term in advertising circles, much favoured no doubt by the creatives themselves!

BECTU, an important trade union in the broadcasting business, and the Inland Revenue use the term *grade* to distinguish the various distinct jobs within sectors. I suspect this is a remnant of film industry parlance. It simply means *category*, which is perhaps a less hierarchical term.

Finally, the use of the term *employer* is sometimes a little problematic. Throughout this book I have used the word simply to mean the person who pays the freelance as well as the usual meaning as the person (or corporate body) with whom the employee has a contract of employment. The first chapter will make it quite clear that *employer* has a strict legal meaning and is used to define or describe a relationship with an *employee*, which again has a strict and distinct legal meaning. This dual use of the word *employer* is perhaps not entirely satisfactory but I do not believe that there is a practical alternative. It should be quite clear from the context when I am using the term in its strict legal context and when I am referring to the person who engages the services of the freelance.

I think I have a duty to give as clear a picture of the life of a freelance as I can. I have tried to do this, and it has inevitably meant saying quite a lot about the problems and disadvantages of a freelance career. If it seems at times that these appear to outweigh the advantages and satisfactions of freelance work, this is not my intention. It is not easy to find work in the audio-visual industries, permanent contracts of employment are highly sought after, and if you really want to work in this industry, you might have no choice but to become a freelance. It is important that you understand what this entails, both the good and the bad. My hope is that, by reading it, this book will help you to avoid or minimise the bad and enjoy the good.

1
What is a freelance?

freelance: anyone who works for himself or herself, employed or paid by others only for particular, usually short-term, assignments.

The Chambers Dictionary 1993

The dictionary definition of the freelance is deceptively simple. It goes to the heart of the matter by talking about short-term assignments and that's what, at its simplest, being a freelance is all about – working on a particular project until it is finished – and then moving on. Like most things in life, however, things are not quite as simple as they first appear and a simple dictionary definition is not going to get us very far in an understanding of freelancing in the audio-visual industries. The aim of this chapter (and in some ways of the whole book) is to arrive at an understanding of just what a freelance is, what a freelance does and how a freelance does it. To do this we will need to look at the idea of the freelance from a number of different points of view. In this way we may come to an understanding of what is involved in actually being or becoming a freelance.

The term *freelance* is used widely and, it has to be said, very loosely. Its meaning can and does change depending on the speaker and on the nature of the conversation. Let's take one or two examples.

FREELANCE MEANS BEING UNEMPLOYED (OR ALMOST)

For some the expression suggests thinly disguised unemployment. Just as an actor might describe himself as *resting* if he has no work, so a director might describe himself as a freelance if his income stream is intermittent, unreliable or simply non-existent. In other words, freelance may mean that you aspire to work in some capacity in the audio-visual industries, but you haven't actually got a job.

FREELANCE MEANS FREEDOM TO CHOOSE

At the other end of the spectrum, some of our most distinguished media professionals would describe themselves as freelance and it would be very surprising if their income stream was intermittent or unreliable! In a recent interview, correspondent Rageh Omaar talked about his decision to leave the employment of the BBC. He said: 'It just made sense to go freelance; most of the *names* at the BBC are freelance.'[1] The reason for his decision was the freedom that his freelance status would give him to pursue his interests across a broad field of activity in both journalism and television production.

FREELANCE MEANS YOU HAVE NO CHOICE

For many, if not most, new and aspiring entrants to the industry, the freedom to choose a project or to choose an employer is an undreamed of luxury. Reality and experience suggest that if you are determined to work in broadcasting, freelancing may be the only way to develop a career if offers of permanent employment are not forthcoming. A great deal of evidence suggests that most freelances and certainly those in the early part of their working lives are freelance of necessity and not by choice. Having chosen radio or television as their preferred field of work, they have been obliged to develop a freelance career because they have been unable to secure a permanent contract of employment.

FREELANCE IS THE ONLY OPTION

Of the many freelances I have spoken to in the preparation of this book, I can't recall a single individual under the age of about fifty who wouldn't prefer to be permanently employed. That is not to say that they are not happy and fulfilled in their chosen field, indeed most of them regard themselves as privileged to work in an industry where variety, change and often excitement and travel may well be an accepted and expected part of the daily landscape. For most people, though, the ideal seems to be to secure a permanent full-time job with a major employer like the BBC, ITV, an independent production company or a facilities house.

FREELANCES IN CONTEXT

Freelances in a changing industry

There have always been freelances in the broadcasting industry. In the past these were often specialist workers with particular craft skills. So, for example, a costume designer, much in demand for specific skills in, say, seventeenth-century clothing, would be needed for a particular drama. This designer might then move on from a BBC series to a commercial cinema production. Similarly a wildlife cameraman (and in those days they usually *were* men) might be engaged for a programme which called for his particular skills and experience. These might include the ability to locate, track and film big game in Africa. When the programme ended, the cameraman would move on to other work quite possibly with a different company. Freelancing was, for these few, a way of specialising, of doing only the work they particularly wanted to do and of continuing to hone and develop their particular skills. Because of such specialisation, and the demand for their skills (even if for concentrated but limited periods), these freelances often commanded higher wages than their employed counterparts, and this *percentage lift* (as it was known in the BBC) more than compensated for lack of pension, holiday and other benefits. Today this kind of specialist freelancing is still common, though probably only a small proportion of all freelance employment.

Until relatively recently, however, and certainly well into the 1980s, if you worked in broadcasting then in all probability you would have been permanently employed by one of a small number of major employers, most of whom would have been recognised as household names. These would have been the BBC, ITV companies like Granada or TVAM or independent local radio stations like Capital or Radio Clyde. This period of relative stability in the structure and operation of the broadcasting industry (and in patterns of employment in the sector) rapidly gave way to a period of unprecedented change and upheaval. The 1990 Broadcasting Act imposed on the BBC and ITV companies a duty to commission 25 per cent of programming from independent production companies (known in the trade as *Indies*).

This consolidated the market for independently produced programmes which had already been established by the launch of Channel 4 in 1982. Channel 4 was set up as a commissioner as opposed to a producer of television. As a result of these changes, the independent production sector expanded rapidly. Small and often financially insecure companies proliferated, competing for a share of available commissions. Any employment from these companies usually lasted as long as the commission and contracts were often issued on a month-by-month or commission-by-commission basis. This pattern of employment continues to be the norm.

As the independent sector grew, internal changes in the UK's biggest broadcaster, the BBC, also had a profound effect on employment practices. *Producer Choice* introduced an internal market to the corporation. This gave BBC producers the ability to choose between internal BBC suppliers of services and outside companies. It was now possible for a series filmed by a BBC crew to be edited outside in a facilities house. Similarly 'outside' crews could be hired and graphics facilities bought-in. In this way the BBC sought both to reduce costs and to transfer business risk and uncertainty to outside companies. Sometimes by choice, often by redundancy, many technical, craft and production staff left the BBC. They either set up their own businesses offering their services to the BBC and others, or went to work for such facilities.

It will be obvious even from this necessarily brief overview that, as a result of these far-reaching structural changes, patterns of employment in the broadcasting industry changed too. This has been described as the *casualisation* of employment in the sector. The echo of the expression *casual labour* is quite deliberate and reflects concern about the short-term nature of many engagements and the vulnerability and lack of security experienced by many, especially (but by no means exclusively), at the outset of their careers. This then is the world of work to which the freelance aspires.

A conservative estimate suggests that every year 3,000 young people leave British universities with media studies degrees of one kind or another. No doubt similar if not greater numbers leave institutions of further education with varying qualifications in this broad subject area. Obviously, not all these young graduates will be seeking careers in media-related employment. Equally obvious, however, is the fact that many graduates from other disciplines will also be looking for a job in radio or television. Whatever the precise statistics might be, common sense and experience lead to one conclusion – that jobs in the media industries are highly sought-after and that competition is fierce. Most students graduate in early summer just at the point when many companies offering the potential of work are preparing to wind down their business operations for the summer whilst their crews and managers are on the road making programmes. This is not an especially good time for recruitment. Sterner commentators will point out that preparations for employment should have started well before graduation, and so they should, but other preoccupations may well have intervened to disrupt this best of all possible worlds! For whatever reason, the search for employment may not have been successful and, like the majority of their contemporaries, recent graduates will find themselves competing with each other for jobs.

FREELANCE – FOR AND AGAINST

The choice between freelance employment and permanent employment is probably in many cases illusory – there just isn't a choice and in the absence of the offer of a permanent contract of employment an individual may well decide to put together a career made up of a series of short-term contracts. This may well be the only way to begin to make progress in the world of television and radio across a wide range of skills and crafts. Indeed, in some areas of work, such as the craft areas of television, work like that of scenic artists and production buyers is traditionally seen as a freelance occupation. So, early in their career, an individual may not have any choice in the matter of freelance as against permanent employment. It is therefore essential to understand the pros and cons of life as a freelance, and to enter the industry with eyes wide open to the perils and pitfalls, as well as the prospects and pleasures of the career which lies ahead. It's worthwhile listing some of the advantages and disadvantages of life as a freelance compared with having a permanent contract of employment.

The case for freelance employment

Freedom – one of the most frequently quoted advantages of freelance work is that it allows the freelance freedom to choose. As a freelance you can choose your employer. There may be companies you like to work with, and by the same token, others you are not so keen on. Essentially the choice is yours. Similarly, you will probably know who is going to be in the crew for any particular job, and again you have a choice; you may wish to work with certain people and not with others. Probably most important is the ability to choose the projects you work on; you may accept some and not others according to your taste and aptitude.

Control – many freelances value the ability to control and direct their own careers. This means that they can try to secure work that will provide them with opportunities to further their expertise and experience in certain fields. In this way they do not depend on line managers who may (quite properly) have their own ideas and agendas in terms of the deployment of the people they manage. By exercising control over your career development, for example, you might decide that you wish to take less work on, say, highly formatted day-time television projects and seek more experience in one-off documentary making. You may decide you would like to move to a completely different genre of programme, perhaps from factual to drama. If you are freelance, you may be able to effect a gradual change from one to the other by a careful choice of projects.

Fast-track your career – some freelances point out that the degree of control over your career (as already discussed) may also mean that you have the opportunity to pursue engagements at an increasingly senior level more rapidly than if you were an employee. Experience gained in one context can be used straight away to justify a higher degree of responsibility in succeeding contracts. A full-time employee will, of course, have to wait until such opportunities arise within the company, or consider moving to another job.

Flexibility – being freelance means that if you enjoy change, or experience the need to change for a variety of reasons, you are able to do so relatively easily. A personal relationship might mean that one partner has more limited choice than the other and needs to go where an employer directs. A freelance partner might more easily accommodate such changes without major upheaval or disruption. Younger freelances without complicating family responsibilities might well value the ability to be flexible in terms of geographical location and to work in different areas of the country or to venture abroad in search of work. You would of course be wise to check on the availability of such work and the legal requirements to be met before you are able to take up offers of freelance work abroad.

Specialisation – it is arguably easier to specialise in certain chosen areas if you are freelance. If you have an interest (or a degree) in archaeology, for example, you could begin to fashion a career as a specialist camera operator (or director, researcher, etc.) on relevant programmes and create a demand for the specialist insight, perspective or skill that you bring to the project, in addition to the sector skill for which you are engaged. It is easy to think of a variety of areas which could lend themselves to the development of specialist work.

Variety – is the other side of the coin to specialisation. Some freelances particularly value the fact that, in moving from project to project, they are not confined to narrow fields of interest but experience new horizons and new demands on their skills on an almost daily basis. Again, as a freelance, it is possible to ensure this variety by exercising control over the work you undertake. If you are employed, then it is the employer or the manager who makes such decisions.

Lifestyle – one freelance editor I spoke to when researching this book was particularly enthusiastic about the ability that freelance work gave him time to pursue other activities which were important in his life. He was able to work hard for months without taking many holidays and then spend prolonged periods with his young family or make extended trips abroad. Freelance work also made it possible for him to develop programme ideas and scripts, thus moving from one kind of work to a very different kind, from one skill to another.

The case against freelance employment

It is vitally important that if you are considering freelance employment in the audio-visual industry that you do so with your eyes wide open. You need to consider the down side and the disadvantages that come with the freelance territory.

Lack of employment security – employers have to think carefully before they make employees redundant or even sack them and the rights of employees are protected by law. There is no such protection for the freelance once the job in hand is finished. Depending on the contract you have, it is probably quite easy to dispense with your services even before the project is completed. In such circumstances it could be difficult to establish that your treatment has offended against any employment laws or regulations or that you have been the victim of any kind of unfair treatment. It is much more difficult in the case of the freelance to decide whether any particular individual receives the protection of laws which specifically state their intention of protecting the rights of *employees*.

Lack of career coherence – we've already seen that as a freelance you enjoy a great deal of freedom to pursue the career you want. However the opposite side of the coin is that when one job ends you have to make a decision. If you need to move straight on to another job (and most people do simply to keep earning) you may have to accept work which you feel is less suitable for you. In other words you can only choose from the range of work on offer at the particular moment when you are free to seek another engagement. Virtually every freelance has faced the frustrating and aggravating situation of having accepted work and then within a few days being offered something more interesting, lucrative or extensive and having to turn it down. Some employers can be very generous if this happens, and agree to release a freelance if the engagement is at a very early stage. Clearly however, this is not always possible or practicable and the freelance will have to take a long-term view.

Lack of financial security – is the consequence of an inability to predict income patterns and the flow of paid work. The seriousness of this insecurity depends very much on individual circumstances but will obviously be more acute if you have significant financial commitments and family responsibilities.

Vulnerability limits choice – well established freelances may possibly pick and choose the jobs they like, though there are probably only a few who can afford such a luxury. Those who are less experienced will be tempted to take whatever work is offered for fear of being unable to find alternatives should they refuse the first job that comes along. This is a particular problem at the start of a freelance career. Many freelances of several years standing are still haunted by the fear that their work will dry up if they begin to refuse work that doesn't really appeal to them.

Vulnerability limits bargaining power – the more you experience lack of security and anxiety about the continuity of work, the less able you will feel to negotiate a good deal in terms of pay and conditions for the work you are offered. Bargaining is more easily done from a position of strength. It is certainly not unknown for employers to exploit younger and less experienced freelancers and to pay less than the going rate for the job. If you need to be convinced about the validity of this point, you only need to look at one or two of the freelance websites for the evidence. Freelances are being encouraged to share information about fees paid by various sectors of the industry to try to strengthen their hands when they negotiate their own fees.[2]

Lack of sick pay and retirement provision – might be a problem for the individual who is concerned about sickness or retirement. If you are a freelance then you will need to take responsibility for these areas on your own shoulders. That of course means responsibility for paying premiums as well as for suitable cover. Most employers will continue to pay full salary to employees if they are unable to work because of illness and this may continue for six months or a year before payments are reduced. If freelances do not work, they are not paid. The self-employed are not entitled to statutory sick pay but are able to claim incapacity benefit from the Department for Work and Pensions through the local benefits office.

Lack of training provision – most employers in the larger organisations provide training courses for their staff and make time available for such courses to be undertaken. This is an area of concern for freelances who not only have to find time to undergo training, but usually have to pay for it too. If freelances do not invest in training they are in danger of having outmoded skills and being uninformed about current equipment and procedures.

Making your mind up

You may find the last section a little disconcerting and negative, especially in a book which is aiming to help those who are considering a freelance career in the audio-visual industry. I think it is very important that you are able to make a decision based on as much information as possible, even if that information makes uncomfortable reading some of the time. What should be emerging is a clearer picture of the professional life of a freelance worker including the stress and strain as well as the satisfaction and success. I think a number of people drift into freelance work because they haven't had success in obtaining a staff position. One thing above all should emerge from reading this book and that is that there is a decision to be made, a decision that should be made with the help of as much information as possible. If you don't like running a small business, if security is really important to you, if you like being a team player in a large organisation, if financial security is one of your top priorities then maybe you should think twice about becoming a freelance – it may not be for you. On the other hand if you can't possibly imagine doing anything other than working in radio or television; if you really can motivate yourself; if you find unpredictability in your life to be a plus rather than a minus; then the life of the freelance may suit you very well.

THE OFFICIAL CONTEXT

It's both interesting and significant to note that, despite its widespread use, the term *freelance* has no legal significance. Yet nothing could be more important for the freelance than a clear definition of the various terms used to describe employment. Such an understanding is crucial because an individual's employment status will affect every part of their lives. This includes not only their working lives but far beyond, and will include their holidays, health, pensions, security and retirement.

At the heart of any understanding of the term *freelance* is the notion that the individual moves from job to job; from employer to employer on a project-by-project, programme or series basis.

EMPLOYED AND SELF-EMPLOYED

Here we look for guidance to the UK Inland Revenue, the government tax agency. The word *guidance* is used here advisedly. The question is ultimately one of law and as such is defined by legislation and the courts, including industrial tribunals. The Revenue defines an individual as *employed* or *self-employed*, that is, the Revenue will take a view on the matter and will naturally wish to see that view prevail. It is important to understand that a decision made by the Inland Revenue regarding employment status may be questioned or challenged and ultimately decisions will be made by the courts. This is, of course, a serious and probably difficult course and one only to be undertaken with professional advice. Essentially when deciding if a person is employed or self-employed, the test is one of control:

- who controls what work is done?

- who controls how and where the work is done?

- is sickness and holiday pay provided?

- who pays the wages and deducts the tax and national insurance (NI) contributions?

If these matters are the responsibility of the employer, then the person is said to be *employed*. On the other hand if an individual is responsible for the payment of income tax and national insurance contributions, then that person is defined as *self-employed*.

Employed

From the Inland Revenue's point of view, if you have a permanent contract of employment then you are considered to be an employee. In this case the employer deducts tax on a Pay As You Earn (PAYE) basis; similarly, National Insurance (NI) contributions are deducted direct from wages or salary. The employer has the responsibility to pass these payments to the Inland Revenue. Shortly after the 5 April (the end of the tax year) the employer is obliged to give each employee a form known as a P60 which details the salary paid over the year which has just ended, and accounts for tax and national insurance payments which have been deducted. Incidentally this form will usually contain details of other deductions from salary like pension contributions. The P60 will also list extra payments such as bonuses which might have been made.

From time to time, the employee will receive, direct from the Inland Revenue authorities, a notice of coding which explains exactly the rate at which tax will be deducted from their salary or wages. This is necessary because each individual's personal circumstances vary, and therefore the rate at which tax is deducted will vary too. Marital status and dependent children, for example, will affect the amount of money allowed before tax is deducted. These are known as personal allowances. Similarly, other income may be taken into consideration; this too will affect the code applied to the taxing of income from employment. In the simplest cases, this will be the limit of the employee's contact with the tax authorities and the employed individual who has no other sources of income other than a weekly or monthly salary will not even be required to complete a self-assessment tax return.

Employed status clearly offers many benefits which are not available to the self-employed or freelance. As we have already seen, if you have a permanent contract of employment, then the employer takes the responsibility for operating the tax system of your behalf. The benefits of the status of employee extend far beyond this. Job security may be an important factor when considering a freelance career, and clearly the importance of this will vary from individual to individual. Attitudes to job security will vary not only according to the personality of the individual but according to personal circumstances as well. A young person with few responsibilities may well take a rather more relaxed attitude to the issue of job security than an older person with responsibilities for young children or older relatives. Planning for the future may well affect attitudes to employment. Most employers will offer pension schemes and more importantly make significant contributions to them. The freelance is left to make private arrangements for such provisions and will have to finance them personally too.

Self-employed

If you do not have a permanent contract of employment, or if fixed-term contracts issued to you are for periods of less than nine months, then you are deemed by the Revenue to be self-employed. In this case you are responsible for paying tax and national insurance to the Inland Revenue, usually through the self-assessment system. Figures are collected through the self-assessment form completed every year and payments are collected on an annual basis, although payments on account (in other words *in advance*) will usually be required half-way through the tax year, in July. Even from this very brief outline, it will be immediately apparent that the self-employed person takes on all the responsibility for tax and national insurance issued in addition to arranging for pension and other matters.

Self-employed freelance (Schedule D freelance)

By now it should have become clear that a freelance is usually self-employed in the view of the Inland Revenue. In fact being freelance can be seen as one type of self-employment. The relationship between a self-employed plumber and the client householder is obviously significantly different in a number of ways to that which exists between a freelance researcher and a production company, yet both plumber and researcher are self-employed. It is essential that the freelance and the intending freelance understand that they are self-employed, because this status in the eyes of the law brings responsibilities and obligations; neglecting or ignoring them can attract unwelcome penalties and difficulties. It is, however, important to understand that it is ultimately the Inland Revenue that will decide on the status of each individual. Because the self-employed are responsible for handling their own taxes and may offset their expenses against their tax liabilities, the revenue operates a fairly strict policy on the grades (or jobs within the media sector) that it will define as self-employed. Even here, the definition may well change from contract to contract, depending for example on whether or not (as in the case of camera operators) the contract requires substantial provision of equipment or whether the work is done away from the premises of the person who engages them. In certain cases, where a worker not covered specifically by these rules has successfully made a case to the Inland Revenue that they should be regarded as self-employed, they will be issued with a letter to be shown to those who engage them confirming their status. By now it will be clear that this is a complex area and requires care on the part of the freelance to comply with the rules. The Inland Revenue makes guidance notes available for the television industry and these can be found on the tax authority's website.[3]

Employed freelance (PAYE freelance)

As a general rule it can be assumed that freelance status will mean that the individual is deemed by the Inland Revenue to be self-employed, and therefore will take on responsibility for the payment of tax and the keeping of expenses records. In some circumstances, however, it is possible for a freelance to be treated as employed for the purposes of PAYE.

Why employment status is important

It's important to understand from the outset that the precise legal conditions under which work or employment is undertaken is crucial in determining the rights of the individual in the workplace. Major employers like the BBC will make these conditions clear in their contracts of employment. The range of benefits available to a BBC employee on a permanent contract is enormous. In addition to the areas of salary, sick pay and holidays, employees are able to access a raft of provisions from car schemes to counselling and financial advice.[4] On the other hand, the freelance will have to check very carefully to discover which benefits (if any) are available when the contract of employment is not permanent. Fortunately the task of finding this information may not be as difficult as it first appears. Major corporations like ITV companies and the BBC make the terms of their contracts for freelances generally available for scrutiny and each freelance will, of course, be provided with a contract of employment making these conditions clear. Many independent production companies are members of a trade association, PACT (Producers' Alliance for Cinema and Television). Pact has negotiated terms and conditions for the employment of freelances. Each member of PACT in effect agrees to implement this agreement and to adhere to its contents. The agreement was negotiated with BECTU, one of the principal trades unions in the media sector. This agreement is highly detailed and wide ranging, and covers freelances in most categories of radio and television. As is usual in these cases, members of PACT will implement this agreement regardless of whether the freelance is a member of BECTU or not. Because of the vulnerability and insecurity which are often the experience of many freelances, serious consideration should certainly be given to union membership. This issue is dealt with at greater length in Chapter 2.

The worker

Recent developments in European employment law have had a direct impact on the UK legal position, especially in the area of workers' rights. Indeed the very term *worker* is one that the legislation seeks to promote. In determining rights, responsibilities and benefits, the law now deals with the *worker* rather than with the *employed* or *self-employed*. (It should be noted that in terms of tax the crucial definition remains that of employed and self-employed.) Essentially a *worker* is defined as anyone who is not in business on their own account. By this definition a staff sound-recordist working for an ITV company on a permanent contract and a freelance sound recordist who moves from company to company on short-term contracts could both be defined as *workers* with the same protection under the law. This concern with precise definition may at first seem a little theoretical and legal-istic, but a second glance reveals that important rights and protection may now be available to many freelances. As a self-employed person there will be no entitle-ment to holiday pay, sickness pay and minimum rest periods between shifts and eligibility for redundancy payments. The Employment Rights Act of 1996, however, makes it possible for freelances who carry out work personally and who work under close supervision to argue the case for being considered to be workers and, in doing so, to gain from the benefits that the legislation guarantees. Significantly, many companies employing freelances in the audio-visual industries have changed their previous position and now give entitlements to paid holidays.

A freelance worker is a business-person

A freelance worker who is recognised by the Inland Revenue as self-employed needs to keep business records, engage in book-keeping, send out invoices and statements and account for all these matters to agencies like the Inland Revenue and Customs and Excise (VAT). There may be a requirement to buy and finance equipment, and to obtain insurance for what has been bought along with many other day-to-day but equally important issues requiring attention. The freelance is in effect running a small and possibly very demanding business and therefore needs to carry out many of the activities that any other business will engage in. It's absolutely essential to understand from the outset that your freelance status unavoidably involves you in running a small business. Like any other small business, operating as a freelance requires planning and needs systems, however modest, to be put in place in a timely way to avoid difficulties and possibly disasters later down the line.

A more detailed account of some of the more important aspects of running this kind of small business is dealt with later in Chapter 8.

AN INDUSTRY PERSPECTIVE

The freelance profile

This chapter has been all about trying to find out what a freelance is, and what a freelance does. So far, however, we haven't really looked at the data that's available to us. From it we can put together a fairly sharp and accurate picture. The Skillset Freelance Survey published in January 2002 tells us that:

- two-thirds of freelances are men.

- 7.6 per cent are of ethnic minority origin.

- the average age is 39, though the age profile of women is much lower, with 56 per cent aged 35 or under.

- over one-quarter of them have a media studies degree; a further quarter have a degree in another subject.

- 15 per cent have a postgraduate degree in a media-related subject.

- in financial terms, a third of freelances earned less than £20,000 in the preceding year, though 10 per cent of the men earned more than £50,000.

- 60 per cent of freelances live in London or the South East.[5]

This then is the freelance in the audio-visual industry; a demanding, rewarding and in many ways privileged occupation. The freelance world is a tough, hardworking world too and has more than its fair share of disappointment and difficulties. Yet despite the problems, it's a world which every year, thousands want to join and in which even more thousands seek to prosper. Finding out how you start a career and then how you can sustain it will occupy our next two chapters.

2
Starting a freelance career

Nice work if you can get it,
And you can get it if you try.
Ira Gershwin,
'Damsel in Distress' (1937)

The title of the preceding chapter, *What makes a freelance?* suggests that there are some important distinctions between a freelance worker and an employed worker in the television and radio sectors of the audio-visual industries. Needless to say this goes beyond simply doing a good job; you are bound to do that to the best of your ability regardless of the status of your employment. But there is something different about being, say, a freelance camera operator as opposed to being a camera operator employed by a production company or broadcaster. This chapter sets out to deal with the qualities which are required in a special way by those engaged in a freelance career. Most of the readers of this book will either be contemplating a freelance career, or in the early stages of developing one, so this chapter will look at ways to begin a freelance career. Just as beginnings are important, finding ways to maintain and to develop a career are just as vital, if not more so; otherwise a promising career may stagnate or even stall. Chapter 3 will go on to look at ways of maintaining, developing and building freelance careers.

EDUCATION AND QUALIFICATIONS

It is very difficult to make broad generalisations about the educational qualifications you need to work as a freelance or, indeed, as a permanent employee in the audio-visual industries. There is a huge range and variety of work available, some requiring a high degree of technical expertise and recognised qualifications. Other work demands aptitudes and abilities. Apart from some engineering and craft occupational categories, it would be true to say that, in radio and television, education is probably more important than qualification. What I mean is that an ability to think clearly, to look for information and to know where to look for it, along with a good range of interpersonal skills, are really going to count in the business. When the BBC recruits for its training schemes, it has this to say:

Trainees are recruited according to their talent, potential and passion to achieve great things with us, rather than their formal academic backgrounds.

This isn't suggesting that academic education is not important, but it does suggest that the fact that you *have* studied is possibly more important than *what* you have studied. A university degree or college certificate or diploma shows that you have the ability, self-discipline and motivation to follow a course and see it through to the end. Towards the end of the previous chapter we saw that about half of all freelances have some kind of degree, so this is clearly an important starting point. Nevertheless there are many people in the audio-visual industries who have no formal qualifications and who do very well. However, they may well have had to spend quite a lot of time developing particular skills and experience to compensate for the lack of formal training. This is something you may need to bear in mind if you are uncertain about whether you want to go to college or university. Unless you have a very strong conviction that you wish to enter an occupation within broadcasting that does require particular qualifications, it is probably wise to study something that really engages and interests you, in such circumstances you are more likely to learn more and profit from your education. In its turn, this will mean that you have more to offer to a potential employer. There are few jobs which are done exclusively by freelances. This means that if you need to know what qualifications are usually required in a specific occupational group you can learn a lot from job advertisements for full-time vacancies even if you want to be a freelance. Some basic research of this kind will soon make clear the education and experience which are usually needed for a particular job.

The media studies debate

One of the questions most frequently asked by young people who have ambitions to work in the audio-visual industry is: 'Do I need a media studies degree?' The answer to that particular question is simple and it's 'No – you don't need a media studies degree.' The question is so simply answered because it's the wrong question. 'How helpful is a media studies degree in finding employment?' is a far more interesting question and the answers are more interesting to you if you are seriously contemplating work in the media either as a permanent employee or as a freelance.

Skillset figures derived from their 2003 workforce survey indicate that more than half had either obtained or were studying for an undergraduate degree and 21 per cent for a postgraduate degree. About 15 per cent of the undergraduate degrees and 9 per cent of postgraduate degrees were in a media-related subject. (These figures are based on the assumption that none of the respondents held more than one degree at the same level.)

Freelance data from 2002 was collected on a slightly different basis and respondents indicated their *highest* qualification gained or currently being studied. Interestingly the data indicates that over half are graduates and a further 29 per cent have a postgraduate qualification (or are studying for one). Over half of both types of degree are in media-related subjects.[6]

It seems that media-related qualifications are more prevalent amongst freelances than in the industry as a whole. The reasons for this are unclear especially as the data for the two groups are rather differently derived. It is clear however that a very large proportion of graduates working in the audio-visual industry have media-related qualifications, and that in terms of freelance employment there are more media graduates than graduates of all other subjects put together. That this should be so is hardly surprising and somewhat gives the lie to those who constantly detract from the value of media studies as a proper subject of academic study. This fashionable habit of *knocking* media studies is all the more disturbing as it so often emanates from those working in elevated positions in the media who really should know better. They should be more careful to establish their arguments on the facts and not on uninformed prejudice.

It is surprising that the study of the media, radio, television, the press and the new digital media should need any defence at all. Few would doubt the power of such forms of communication to influence events and lives round the globe. A clear understanding of how the media work and the mechanisms by which they exert their influence must be of the profoundest importance in a responsible society. If critics wish to criticise particular courses or schemes of study, fair enough, no one would wish to defend poor teaching or enquiry that is not rigorous. I am not sure however that such criticism is what lies behind the onslaught against media studies. Instead it seems to smack of intellectual elitism and snobbery. It's comforting to remember that not so long ago, the study of the novel was thought to be unworthy of serious attention! The media should be the subject of serious academic enquiry for its own sake and because such enquiry is important and significant.

Many undergraduates on media studies courses have no intention of applying for jobs in the media and go on to work in a variety of other fields. It is however worth pointing out that they do go on to work! Recent figures compiled by the Association of Graduate Careers Advisory Services indicate that, six months after graduation, media studies graduates have some of the highest employment rates.[7]

These findings have also been confirmed and strengthened by a three-year study led by the University of Sunderland and involving four universities with large media studies departments.[8]

So if we are still asking if a media studies degree helps, then it is clear that it's one of the best degrees to have if you want to find work, whether it's in the media or not.

The advantages of a media studies degree

The main advantages of a degree of any kind consist in the benefits that academic study brings; the ability to reason logically, to pursue enquiry and to be guided by fact and not assumption or prejudice. Additionally the ability to express and present oneself in writing as well as in person, and a degree of confidence in doing so are important outcomes of a good course. It can be argued that the precise course of study is ultimately of less importance, though of course this depends very much on your intended employment. A degree in politics or international relations may be of enormous value to you if you want to work in the reporting or production of current affairs, news or documentaries. In such circumstances such a degree may well be of far more value ultimately than a media studies degree. In many cases, however, the situation may be far less clear and an undergraduate may simply know that he or she would like to pursue a career in some sector of the audio-visual industry. The scope may of course be even wider and include an interest in public relations or advertising, for example. There are some clear advantages that a degree in media studies will bestow, including:

- an understanding of the nature and structure of the media industries;

- a knowledge of the ownership and control of the media;

- a study of the impact and influences of the media on society;

- a study of media texts and structures.

In addition, depending on the course of study, more practical production elements may give an insight into:

- editorial decision-making;

- pitching and programme proposals;

- health and safety;

- audio-visual recording techniques;

- editing.

In conclusion, it is hard to see how an education which includes some or all of these elements could fail to provide a good starting point for work in the audio-visual industry. No degree will guarantee you work in the media, but the figures I've already referred to speak for themselves. A degree or other qualification is a help, but a media studies degree is hard to beat when it comes to securing work, freelance or not.

Choosing a course

If you do decide to choose a media studies degree, there's a wide range of courses available and you may need help to make your decision. There are a number of course guides now available, and in addition you will want to look at each college or university prospectus very carefully for details of what each programme of study includes. Courses tend to range from the almost exclusively academic and theoretical to the very practical and vocational. A small number of institutions (like my own) offer a 'mixed economy' of academic work with short but intense practical production opportunities for those who wish to pursue them. You will have to make your mind up what kind of course would suit you best, but it would be a mistake to assume that because you want to work in the industry you should decide on the most practical or vocationally focused course available. A solid academic understanding of the media can be very helpful in a career in the audio-visual industries. It will be helpful if you can find out:

- what academic units make up the course;

- what specialisations are available;

- how assessments are carried out;

- what research interests the staff of the department have;

- what final year choices exist for dissertations, practical projects or placements.

If your interests extend to practical or production matters you should inform yourself about:

- the nature of practical/production units;

- how many of them are available to undergraduates;

- the kind of recording and editing equipment that is used;

- the number of students who have to share the available equipment;

- how adequate the technical support is to maintain or repair the equipment;

- the availability of previous years' student work for viewing.

In addition, it is helpful, whatever kind of course you choose, to discover:

- the quality of relationships the department has outside the university, for example with broadcasters and other parts of the industry. This will be important even for degrees which are predominantly academic.

- what information is available about the employment of graduates.

- if work experience placements are available, how they are organised and supervised.

New entrants schemes

There are a number of schemes in place to help new entrants gain access to the industry. They tend to be sector-specific so that they can be more effectively geared to the requirements of the particular sector for which they have been set up. These schemes should be thought of as training opportunities and usually follow a curriculum that lasts between one and two years. Entrants or trainees are provided with placements in ongoing productions, they have tasks to accomplish and work alongside industry professionals. In addition, trainees attend specialist short courses which provide backup to the practical skills they are learning. It is very unlikely that any entrant embarking on such a scheme will not be placed in employment at the end of training, though of course no guarantees are offered. Unfortunately, numbers on such schemes are severely restricted and it's estimated that there are no more than 100 places each year for the entire industry across the UK. New entrant training schemes are administered by FT2 in England, by Cyfle in Wales and by Scottish Screen. Details are given in Chapter 10.

Apprenticeships

Apprenticeships in England have been undergoing a period of change. At the time of writing this has resulted in the temporary suspension of the schemes funded by Skillset, apart from a specific photo-imaging apprenticeship. It is assumed that schemes will resume once research has been carried out in order to ensure that apprenticeships fully meet the precise training requirements of the industry. Apprenticeships continue to be offered in Scotland and are set at Level 6 of the Scottish Credit and Qualifications framework.

Apprenticeships are usually available to those without a degree and usually have to be completed between the ages of sixteen and twenty-four. To find out more about the availability of apprenticeships in the audio-visual industry, you would be well advised to contact the agencies listed above in the section on new entrant schemes.

AMBITION

Jon Snow, that doyen of television news presenters, is a regular visitor to the university where I teach. He comes to talk to students and, inevitably, on each of his visits, he's asked about career prospects. As a refreshing change from many industry practitioners speaking from the lofty heights of an established career, he is warmly encouraging of anyone who wishes to take up a career in the industry. Instead of the usual sharp intake of breath and sad shake of the head when talking about employment, he's upbeat and positive in his assessments. 'If you want to do it,' he says, 'you can, you'll find a way.' Many of the freelances and their employers that I've spoken to in recent years would echo these sentiments. However, it's worth looking at two of the deceptively simple words Jon Snow uses in his response, *want* and *find*. Together, what these two words convey is *ambition*.

A great deal of ambition is required to embark on a career in the media industries. The competition for jobs is fierce, and in many ways the freelance or would-be freelance is in effect selling in a buyers' market. Every year, at least 2,000 students graduate in media-related subjects from universities in the UK. In addition, students from other disciplines are also keen to develop media-related careers, and are encouraged by potential employers to do so. Colleges of further education similarly contribute to the numbers seeking media employment, as do those who are either unemployed or are seeking a career change. At this point I have not distinguished between seeking employment on a permanent contract and doing so on a freelance basis. For most people, finding a job, and in particular finding the right job, is one of the most important things they ever do – it's also one of the most challenging, draining and difficult – some might even say traumatic. For some, the challenge of finding employment may only arise once, and as a result they embark on a career with a company in whose employment they will stay for the rest of their working lives. For most, however, a working life will involve the challenge of three of four changes of job or career direction in the course of thirty or forty years' work. By contrast, even the most successful freelance will need to convince a potential employer of their abilities several times a year at least – a daunting prospect indeed. The well-worn phrase 'you're only as good as your last job' may become a haunting and worrying reality!

An ambition to succeed is therefore one of the most important weapons in the armoury of an intending freelance.

DETERMINATION

Lofty ambition or even ambition that is not so lofty is a prerequisite for the life of a freelance, but if ambition is to become reality and not simply remain a dream, determination is perhaps the next most important quality required. Determination is about overcoming setbacks and remaining committed when events suggest that it might be more sensible to give up and try something else. Looking at the life of many freelances starting their careers, it appears to take quite a long time before an individual may have the grounds to feel confident about work prospects for twelve months into the future. That is not to say that contracts have been lined-up or agreed, but that there is a reasonable prospect of having work over that period. In fact, it can often take a new freelance up to two years before a steady and reliable income stream is established. The length of time it takes to establish a career in this way will also depend on the particular skill or craft that the freelance offers. No wonder then that *determination* is such a prerequisite. Many difficult choices lie ahead. Should the freelance take part-time or even full-time employment in another field whilst seeking freelance contracts in the chosen field?

Inevitably the situation will arise in which the individual is forced to choose between ongoing employment in a call-centre, for example, and a short, (possibly very short) contract in the television or radio industry. There are certainly no hard and fast rules in place to resolve such dilemmas. Even a week's work with a production company might be the very opportunity which unlocks the door to a successful career; on the other hand it might not. Tantalisingly of course, even if this week's work does not lead to an immediate offer of future employment, the initial contact could bear fruit many weeks or even months later.

It should have become clear by now that the freelance career involves substantial risks and finely balanced judgments, especially at the outset. Whatever else, life as a freelance requires a certain robustness of character and an ability to stay motivated in difficult circumstances. This ability may well be affected by circumstances not directly related to the chosen career. Family commitments and responsibilities may well militate against the ability to take risks with regular income. No amount of motivation or determination will overcome the responsibility of feeding children or caring for aged parents, for example.

PROFESSIONALISM

Perhaps not surprisingly, this may be the most problematic attribute for the novice freelance, particularly at the end of student days. Higher or further education will hopefully have imparted an ability to think and possibly the ability to communicate. In addition, depending on the course of study undertaken, key technical and production skills may also have been learned. What might not be quite so obvious is the requirement to be professional. To put it as politely as possible, not all intending freelances will have learned the key skills required of those seeking to sell their skills to those who need to engage them. Employers emphasise the need for a number of personal attributes in those they choose to engage. In case I stand accused of trying to promote a personal agenda of old-fashioned Meldrew-like etiquette, I will try to explain, in each case, the professional reasons that such attributes are so highly desirable.

- *Politeness* is essential – most of those who work in television or radio come into contact with individuals who can have a profound influence on the outcome of the task in hand. This might mean members of the public whose cooperation is essential in the making of a programme, or commissioners, executive producers or their representatives whose goodwill is crucial to the future plans of the company. Evidence of impatience, a lack of a sense of humour or an overdeveloped sense of personal dignity may well suggest to a potential employer that such a person is not to be trusted with their project.

- *Punctuality* is highly regarded in an industry which runs by minutes and seconds, and quite often fractions of a second. A freelance who regularly turns up late for appointments or who is unreliable in other matters of time keeping is not likely to feature highly on the wanted list of a producer who is buying satellite time by the minute or second or who regularly works to tight deadlines.

- *Preparedness* is impressive, but its lack can be a fatal flaw in a potential freelance. It can be quite surprising and not a little irritating when someone comes to ask for advice or contacts, lacking a notebook or a pen or pencil. It's hard to take such a person seriously – basically they are looking for a favour but are not prepared to put in a moment's forethought on their side.

EVALUATING YOUR SKILLS

The so-far unspoken assumption lying behind this chapter and, indeed, at the heart of this book is the requirement of the freelance to put a range of skills at the disposal of the employer. The skills required of a particular occupational group will, of course, be dealt with as we go on to look at many of the sectors within the audio-visual industry. I am convinced, though, that the freelance or intending freelance needs to think very carefully about the whole area of skills and what this means for a career. The way you present yourself will depend to a great degree on how you present your skills. So it is well worth spending a little time thinking analytically about your skills. Amongst the questions it would be worthwhile considering are:

- what skills have I already acquired?

- how do I intend to develop and refine these skills?

- what new skills do I intend to acquire now?

- what skills do I intend to acquire in the future?

The way in which you carry out this evaluation or audit of your skills may have an important bearing on your success in your search for freelance work or for your success as you try to enter the freelance market. There are two broad headings under which you will find it useful to carry out this evaluation.

1   What skills do I possess which are directly relevant to my chosen freelance occupation?

2   What other skills do I possess which might be relevant in some way to my work as a freelance?

Most of us are fairly aware of the answer to the first question. Many readers will be completing courses they have chosen to do because of the skills they will acquire to prepare themselves for a particular occupation. The answers to the second question may not be difficult but they may be far less obvious and therefore are in danger of being overlooked. What we are considering here is really the question of transferable skills. These are skills you have acquired throughout your life in all your activities and which you carry forward into your professional, working life. The problem with transferable skills is that you might take them for granted. If you do, you will not mention them to a potential employer and might thereby lose the edge in the competition for work. As you seek to evaluate these skills you should think not only about your formal education and training, but about your hobbies, social activities and interests. Nor should you forget to think about any employment you have already had during vacations, for example. Holiday employment might have been fairly menial, but most jobs are demanding and help to develop skills. Thinking about these areas will no doubt illuminate many of the skills you have and which you might have overlooked. It could also be worth asking someone who knows you well to help with the exercise. The following are areas you might consider when you audit your transferable skills:

- *Communication* – the ability to express ideas, to negotiate, to write clearly.

- *Research and planning* – identifying and gathering information. Problem solving and goal setting.

- *Human relations* – the ability to develop a rapport with others and create cooperation within a group.

- *Organisation and management* – the ability to initiate and generate ideas, define goals and to evolve strategies to achieve them. The ability to motivate others.

These of course are fairly general areas; remember, too, the more specific skills you might have acquired because of your family background, the contacts you have and the languages you speak. What you learn about yourself as you evaluate your transferable skills should inform the way you seek work as a freelance. In preparing a professional CV you should be seeking to demonstrate how these skills, as well as the occupational skills you have, can be of relevance to the project you are seeking to join. As we will discover as we come to think specifically about the CV, this will probably mean a flexible and changing approach and a willingness to adjust the document to make it more relevant to the particular employer you are approaching.

ORGANISATION

It is possibly trite to make the point that the freelance needs to be well organised. But what may be obvious in theory might be far more problematic in practice. By its very nature the life of a freelance will probably be unpredictable and irregular. Most people find it difficult and irksome to manage their bank account, pay bills and simply keep up with all the other routine tasks of daily life. Managing these apparently routine parts of life can become doubly difficult when working hours are irregular and long periods may be spent away from home – often at short notice. Finding a solution to these problems can be more than worthwhile, and if tackled early in a freelance career may well avoid a number of difficulties and hours of wasted time.

Computing

Ownership of a computer should be regarded as essential to the pursuit of a freelance career. Properly set up and used it can be the key to carrying out many routine tasks quickly and efficiently. It can, for example, help to:

- track appointments and give reminders;

- keep accounts;

- carry out online banking;

- produce attractive letters;

- design and maintain a CV;

- generate letterheads and business cards;

- run email;

- design and maintain a website.

You will need to choose appropriate software, usually a suite that will perform most of the functions listed above. Microsoft Office is the industry standard for most of these applications. Microsoft products are packed with features, but they can be an expensive purchase for the freelance. Although it is certainly advisable to ensure that the data and files you produce to share with others are compatible with the most frequently used software, there are other, cheaper programs that offer this compatibility.[9]

It is also essential that you ensure that basic computer housekeeping is carried out on a regular basis. This will of course include keeping anti-virus and firewall software up to date and performing regular backups of all your data. Failure to observe these simple but regular tasks invites catastrophe on a massively time-consuming scale.

The reader will find a more detailed treatment of running the business side of freelance work in Chapter 7.

PRESENTATION

Radio and television professionals spend a great deal of time thinking about how things look and sound; appearances matter in this industry. So the freelance needs to communicate competence and professionalism. There are many ways in which this can be achieved. Basic business stationery can certainly help and is not necessarily expensive. A decent business card which contains essential contact information can help to convey an impression of competence – a scrap of grubby paper may not do the job quite as well. Spending a little time setting up clear and attractive business templates in your word-processing software will provide you with letterheads, compliments slips and other stationery without the expense of having them professionally printed. The emphasis should be on the business-like and you would be advised to be cautious and possibly a little conservative in your designs; there is no point losing work simply because your potential client doesn't share your taste for art deco design. Above all, the material you produce should be clear, informative and uncluttered.

The CV or résumé

For most people, the CV or résumé is something they use only a few times in their lives. On the other hand the freelance, especially in the early stages of a career, will make frequent use of it by way of introduction and in order to catalogue the expertise and experience that is offered. It follows then that a significant priority is to keep the CV up to date. In any case, care should be taken to make sure that it never lags more than about a month behind. It may be helpful to remember that you can have more than one version of your CV available and that each version can be tailored to the particular market you are attempting to address. You may find that you wish to emphasise certain aspects of your experience and expertise to engage the interest of a small independent production company whilst giving a slightly different gloss to a major broadcaster. You may well, for example, be looking for different kinds of work. It might be appropriate to look for work as a camera *operator* in the corporate sector and at the same time seek engagements as a camera *assistant* for broadcast work. You may feel that you could work as a producer/director for a programme on a locally transmitted opt-out programme but would realistically aim for researcher/director work on a nationally transmitted network production. I am not for a moment suggesting any kind of deception – indeed there is no quicker way to get a bad reputation in the industry than exaggerating experience and ability. I am suggesting however that in the busy world of television and radio production it may be advisable to use CVs that are tailored to the purpose for which they are required. Additionally it is worth considering what kind of information a potential client requires. When a candidate applies for a permanent post, a CV is important because it is a statement of educational, work and personal history. A freelance CV, however, plays a rather different role and whilst it should include basic background information it will put far more emphasis on production credits, experience and qualifications. It is also worth giving some thought to skills you may possess which are not directly related to the media. A good command of a specified foreign language might be very important to a producer who is about to embark on a location filming abroad. Similarly an interest and qualification in diving might also play an important part in securing an engagement and could provide the freelance with a competitive advantage.

There are no absolute rules for writing the CV. What follows is the result of a long history of reading them and a comprehensive trawl through a number of websites and articles, a few of which claim to offer the complete solution. I make no such claims, but pass on some steps and hints to get you started. You will quickly discover what you like best, and more importantly what works best for you.

- *Do it now!* It's amazing how many students about to graduate still haven't prepared their CV or brought it up to date since they prepared one at school. Coming into contact with many freelances I've noticed how those who appear to be most dynamic (and successful) seem able to produce their CV at the drop of a hat. Leaving it to the last minute is fatal. Preparing a good CV takes a little time and shouldn't be rushed, especially when you need quite a lot of detail and you need it to be accurate. Your first shot at a professional document will need you to bring together quite a few bits of paper, so give yourself the time you need to assemble the facts.

- *Do it twice!* This isn't as stupid as it may seem. I'm advising you to prepare two versions of your CV. The first is a comprehensive CV, a complete record in detail of your education and working life. This will always be useful for you to keep, and some employers and institutions will need it. The second version which we might as well call your *professional CV* will be more geared towards your professional freelance experience and your skills for this work. The background facts of your life may be included but only in outline, not in detail. You might mention your school, for example, but you will not need to list all the exams you passed, nor the grades you achieved.

- *Do it on a computer.* This advice is probably unnecessary. As a freelance you will need to bring your CV up to date on a regular basis. At an early stage in your career, many of the steps you take will be significant. Your first work for a major indie or broadcaster will be a milestone and should be included as soon as possible. The only way to ensure that you can do this quickly and efficiently is to keep it live on your computer. Keeping your CV on a computer also makes it easier for you to make the two versions I'm suggesting. The shorter one will of course be based on a copy of the comprehensive CV.

- *Keep a back up.* Following on from the previous point, your CV is almost as important as your passport, in some ways it is the freelance passport. You should keep it safe and you should always know where it is.

- *Put yourself in the employer's shoes.* You will not go very far wrong in writing your professional CV if you constantly remind yourself of who is likely to read it and what they need to know. The most important information should be clearly visible at the first glance. Remembering your intended reader will help you to prioritise the information you offer.

- *Keep it simple.* Like all good writing, simplicity is the key to effective communication on a CV. This is as true for the layout of your document as it is for the words you use and for the construction of your sentences. Remember to use a maximum of two fonts. This is not the time to show off your intimate knowledge of the whole library of TrueType fonts! Nor should you be using colours other than black. Cool and professional is the order of the day; there is no point in putting off a potential employer simply because he or she doesn't like your particular taste in fancy borders or illustrations.

- *Proof-read your work.* The CV is your primary marketing document. It must be accurate and correct. A spell check on your computer will help but it can't find all the mistakes all of us make from time to time. If you type *too* instead of *two*, the word processor will not correct your mistake.

- *Proof-read your work.* This is not a mistake but is simply a repetition of how important it is to check your CV before you send it out. You should be honest enough to know how good your spelling, grammar and syntax are. If they are not as good as they might be, ask someone else to check it over for you. Even if your standards are high it's still worth having someone else cast a fresh pair of eyes over your work. I can spot a spelling mistake or typo in someone else's document at a hundred paces, it will literally leap off the page! I will miss them in my own work because I see what I expect to read, not what is actually on the page.

- *Convey your skills and experience.* These are what your potential employer is looking for. These should be the areas that should leap off the page and claim the attention of the reader. If you are seeking employment as a producer/director, do you need to mention the fact that you manage your local swimming team? The answer is probably not. Unless of course you organised a world tour and got them successfully to the Olympics. Even then, you will remember to emphasise the organisational and administrative skills you deployed in the endeavour because these are the ones relevant to your employer!

- *Keep your layout clear and simple.* Densely filled pages of small type are very off-putting to the reader. Don't be afraid of white space; there should be plenty of it. Your font size should be about 12 pt. Any smaller and it may be difficult to read, any larger and it's shouting at the reader.

We can now turn to look more closely at the contents of your CV. In the two columns below I outline the content for the two kinds of CV I think you need. As I said earlier, you will be wise to make your own mind up as you become more experienced in preparing and using your own document. At the very least you will be able to use Table 2.1 as a checklist to ensure you haven't omitted some vital information.

Table 2.1   What should be in my CV?

Information for a Comprehensive CV	Professional CV
Name	✓
	Role (e.g. sound recordist)
Full contact address including accurate postcode	✓
Telephone number	✓
Email address	✓
Website address	✓
Personal statement, i.e. aims and ambitions	Not required
Professional statement, i.e. main skills and services offered	✓
Qualifications (diplomas and degrees if any)	✓
Skills and abilities	✓
Work history (most recent first)	Only jobs relevant to freelance
Education, i.e. school(s) attended (most recent first)	Probably not required
Educational results (e.g. GCSE grades, etc.) (most recent first)	Not required
Interests and hobbies	Only if specifically relevant
References 1 Personal reference 2 Professional reference	Not really required ✓

A sample professional CV

Mark Stevens

Researcher/Director

27 Discovery Street
Brownbridge
Manchester
M111 7PQ

0161 496 0197   Mobile 07700 900732
mark.stevens@popmail.net
www.markdirect.tv.uk

Mark Stephens has five years' experience as a self-shooting researcher/ director on a wide range of programmes. He has extensive knowledge of the north west of England and is willing to travel wherever work requires.

Qualifications	BSc (Hons) Biological Sciences, Liverpool University Postgraduate Diploma Broadcast Production, Brighton College of Art
Skills and abilities	Specialised in research skills and directing. Full clean driving licence. Qualified and experienced diver. Interest in marine/wildlife issues following university study. Fluent French and some Arabic spoken.
Recent projects	Sep–Nov 2004 Director location sequences *Wildlife Questions*, Tooth and Claw Productions for Five Television.* Jun–Aug 2004 Researcher/Director (self-shoot) *Pet Posers*, Tooth and Claw Productions for The Pet Channel. Nov 2003–May 2004 Researcher/Director *Shoreline*, Knowledge Video Ltd (Sell Through). Sep–Oct 2003 Underwater Video training course (3wks), Marsa Alam, Egypt. May–Jul 2003 Director (self-shoot) *Give it a Try*, Gormless Productions for BBC Northwest.

* You might consider it appropriate to add a line describing the series e.g. 13 X 30' studio-based quiz series with edited inserts.

LOOKING FOR FREELANCE EMPLOYMENT

It is not particularly difficult to locate the best sources of information about employment opportunities in the media sector, and more especially in radio and television. In newspaper terms, the *Guardian* provides a comprehensive listing of employment opportunities in its Monday *Media* section. There's also an online version on the *Guardian* website.[10] Some other newspapers have similar sections, but the *Guardian* is probably unrivalled for its media coverage. The industry also has its own weekly, *Broadcast*, which again provides comprehensive employment listings. It too has an online presence.[11] The reference section in Chapter 10 provides a list of some of the most commonly available listings of employment opportunities, both in print and online.

Industry perspective

The Skillset freelance survey gives a valuable insight into how freelances actually get their first job. You will perhaps not be surprised to know that little more than 20 per cent of respondents gained their first work through a formal advertisement. A rather larger number (27 per cent) found success by approaching an employer directly and a significant 23 per cent found that critical first job through a friend or relative. Table 2.2 gives an indication of all the sources of the first job.

This data reinforces the important part that personal contacts play in securing work, with more than half the jobs being secured in this way. Networking and word of mouth in the widest sense are likely to play a significant role in securing work; every employer will want to make sure that the freelance is up to the job and will use his or her own judgment or that of others whose appraisal can be trusted to make that assessment. The fact that only 3 per cent of respondents attributed their first work to a diarist or agency should not be taken as indicating that such services are ineffective as such, but they are less likely to be useful in this very early stage of a freelance career.

Table 2.2 Source of first job

Source	%
Approached employer	27
Friend or relative	23
Advertisement	21
Employer direct	14
Word of mouth	12
Careers advice	5
Agency or diarist	3
Trade union	2

Source: Skillset Freelance Survey 2002.

Agencies

There are a number of agencies, many of which have an online presence. Here the freelance can upload a CV or compile one online. This entry is then made available to potential employers searching for freelances for a particular project. The freelance is not usually charged for this service; generally the employer pays for membership of the site and the ability to search the database of freelance CVs. Again, it is worth emphasising the importance of keeping such an online CV up to date – a potential employer is not likely to be impressed if your most recent experience is shown to be two years ago!

Advertising

The more experienced freelance may well find it worthwhile to advertise in a freelance directory or production directory. Clearly some caution and common sense need to be exercised here, and care should be taken to ensure that the guide under consideration is a reputable and well-known publication and one genuinely consulted across the industry. Scotland's publication *Film Bang*[12] for example has been established for many years, and is an invaluable source of telephone numbers and contacts across various sectors of industry skills. It too, like many other directories, is available online.

CONTACTS AND NETWORKING

The television and radio industries are very much network based – each geographical area of the country will have its own media haunts and both formal and informal groups. Plugging into these overlapping and interconnected networks is one of the most important activities the freelance and the intending freelance can engage in. It is difficult to give advice on how to network, but it is possible to suggest possible approaches:

- Take care to find out as much as you can about groups and meetings which might be relevant to your interests.

- Target these groups carefully; you will not be able to give time to everything that is going on, so choose carefully.

- Spend time nurturing your contacts, this is not something you can rush.

- Be subtle, nothing is quite as overpowering as a work-hungry freelance eagerly clutching a handful of business cards. If you gain a reputation for button-holing potential employers, they will simply avoid you in order to avoid embarrassment and boredom.

- Be prepared to work. If you have joined a trade union or interest group, one of the best ways of developing contacts is to volunteer and to help. Engaging in common tasks is a good way of getting to know people and forming a bond. Someone who knows you and trusts you is far more likely to offer you work or to tell you if they know of opportunities which might interest you. If you're very lucky, they might even recommend you! Being prepared to engage in the work of the group demonstrates your ability to be a team player, and indicates that you are a giver as well as a taker.

- *Polite persistence* is a phrase well worth remembering. It embodies a recognition that many media employers are extremely busy and however well-intentioned they are, find difficulty allocating time to those trying to start a media career. They may well need tactful reminders to keep promises of work, work-experience, introductions or other kinds of help. There is a delicate middle-path to be walked between tenacity and determination on the one hand and pestering on the other. A strategy is needed to find ways of gaining attention without getting a reputation as a nuisance!

Work experience

The increasing popularity of work experience placements and internships suggest that this is seen not only as part of a continuing process of education but as an important source of contacts for future work, though this cannot of course be taken for granted. Those undertaking such placements should remember that it can be a two-edged sword. Work experience is an unrivalled opportunity for the potential freelance or employee to demonstrate their commitment and enthusiasm as well as their emerging potential. On the other hand, a potential employer can easily spot problems of attitude, reliability and motivation. It should also remain clear that work experience is precisely that; an opportunity to look at the world of work in the media industries from a closer perspective. It is not helpful to see placements in the industry as a chance to lobby for work. Needless to say, an ambitious student will be sensitive to opportunities that might present themselves. At the beginning of a career, an intending freelance might well be asked to help on a 'no pay' basis.

Working for nothing

Opinions vary in the media industry about the merits and the ethics of expecting or even allowing young people (and it generally is young people) to work for nothing. This is a sensitive area. Many people have made a start in very successful careers by offering – almost insisting – on working for free. In a highly competitive and sought after field you can understand why an employer faced with an obviously highly motivated young person, desperate for the experience, finds it hard to refuse an offer to run errands and make the tea simply in return for the chance to 'be around' the production process. Such keenness and enthusiasm, however, is easily exploited. The thoughtful employer will have procedures and structures in place to cope with such requests. Work experience should ideally take place under the supervision and with the agreement of an educational institution or training agency so that a number of issues concerning the interests of the *trainee* can be addressed. Interestingly, it is difficult to find a satisfactory term to describe the person who is working for free. Legally they are certainly not workers, because they are not in receipt of remuneration for the work they do. There is probably no contract of employment either written or implied. On the other hand, it is probably misleading to refer to such a person as a trainee because there is no guarantee of training or formal scheme of training in place. Whilst many students will use their initiative to secure work experience for perhaps a few weeks in vacation time, working for nothing is a rather different matter. A number of important questions should be asked and answered.

- Are health and safety procedures in place to safeguard the well being of the person concerned?

- Is insurance cover in place?

- Have arrangements been made to cover expenses or to help the trainee?

- How is accommodation to be arranged if the trainee is away from home, or is this to be found from the trainee's own pocket?

- Do other workers in the organisation know of the arrangement or are they likely to be hostile to it if they find out?

- Does a relevant trade union have a view on these matters?

It will quickly become apparent that if the answers to these and other questions are not forthcoming or not satisfactory, then far from working for nothing, the trainee could be seen as paying for the experience.

PROFESSIONAL ORGANISATIONS AND UNIONS

It should be clear by now that work as a freelance in the broadcast industries is exciting and rewarding. For most, the rewards far outweigh the disadvantages. Among the disadvantages, however, are some issues which need to be taken seriously. The freelance essentially works alone, moving from project to project and from one group of colleagues to another. This wide and constantly changing circle of professional peers may be one of the attractions of this kind of working lifestyle. On the other hand, the freelance can be seen as potentially vulnerable, and in many ways isolated and lacking the formal and some of the informal support networks that permanent employment often provides. Trade unions and professional organisations can go a long way towards compensating for some of the drawbacks of freelance employment. In addition, it is possible that the individual may gain enormously from membership of such organisations across a very wide range of activities.

Pay and conditions

Rates of pay, fairness and equity in the workplace are important to everyone, and especially to the freelance who, for many reasons, may be particularly vulnerable to poor practice and exploitation. Membership of a trade union can give support and a sense of solidarity to those working as freelances. BECTU is the principal trade union in the broadcasting areas and has always had a strong representation from freelances in its membership. It negotiates directly with broadcast and production employers and is responsible for agreements reached with PACT, the Producers' Alliance for Cinema and Television, which is the trade organisation for independent producers. PACT and BECTU have jointly implemented an agreement covering the employment of freelances which operates to the benefit of all, and not simply those who are members of the union. There is a wide range of benefits provided by membership of a union which goes far beyond conditions of employment and benefits, important though these are. There are a number of freelance websites which compile information about rates of pay so that you can ensure that you are being paid an acceptable rate for a job. Details of some of these sites are provided in Chapter 10.

INDUSTRY PERSPECTIVE

What employers are looking for

I have spoken to a number of employers whilst preparing this book, all of them employ freelances in a wide variety of (mainly production) roles from runners to series producers and production managers. I was very struck by how much respect they had for the freelances they knew and the work they did. They were certainly in no doubt about the significant role freelances played in the success of the programmes they were responsible for and were very conscious of their responsibilities. The managing director of an expanding independent producer put it this way:

> You need to temper young talent with experience. Unless you have an output deal [guaranteed commissions] you can't put a career structure in place. You have to try to be loyal to those who work for you – and you need a lot of commissions to keep that going.

This fluctuating requirement for freelances was underlined by another employer, this time a broadcaster competing for ITV 1 slots. She was at some pains to point out just how her need for freelances changed even week-by-week according to the programmes she had in production:

> This week I have 3 freelances in Glasgow and 8 in London; next week I'll have between 18 and 20 more on the books.

So what were those responsible for hiring freelances looking for? Sometimes the skills are directly related to programme-making:

I'm looking for those who can show a talent for knowing a good story and how to get it, someone who knows what the audience wants.

In other cases personal qualities are emphasised:

Someone who's enthusiastic with a can-do attitude, self starting not clockwatching, above all with a flexible mind-set.

When it came to giving advice on how best to get work, there were no easy answers or formulas to pass on:

There's a lot of serendipity and luck, being in the right place at the right time, yes there are problems of timing.

There were however some strong hints:

I probably get about 10 CVs every day, if they call me up about them, then that can be a pain – I will make time to meet likely freelances.

On the subject of CVs, one criticism was that they were often too vague:

You should show the productions you've been involved in on a year by year basis, honesty is important; you should be specific about exact roles and times.

There was perhaps more than a hint here that at times vagueness in CVs was deliberate and often tried to cover up experience which wasn't all it seemed to be. Even in London, the largest centre of freelance employment, it's still a small world, and being dishonest in accounts of your experience is not to be recommended, it's too easy for prospective employers to check. For those starting a freelance career and looking for first jobs as runners or junior researchers, there was a great deal of encouragement. Asking for work experience was thought to be a good way of making yourself known and showing you can be useful.

I had a call from a . . . graduate looking for work experience. She came in for a couple of weeks. She fitted in and is going to come back in a month's time for a 6 month contract.

FREELANCE PERSPECTIVE

One freelance who's been in the industry for about three years started as a runner in a film company. He now works for a medium-sized independent outside London as a researcher/director. Reflecting on his early experience he said:

Social skills are the most important, it's how you get on, how you work in a team . . . motivating others. If you have an attitude, you're not going to get on. You need ambition; drive is essential, your first year and your first job needs determination. You have to have an ability to multi-task and stay cool under pressure, you must enjoy pressure.

His experience in getting that vital first job is not an uncommon mixture of persistence and being in the right place at the right time:

I rang [an independent production company] to enquire about work, they asked me for a CV which I sent. Nothing happened, so I walked round and cold-called ... I was looking for a runner's job but they had nothing.

He tried another company. . .

I was offered work experience for £50 a week but after a month the first company I had tried rang and offered me six months as a runner.

When asked about the more technical or creative aspects of his work he said:

It helps to have a good eye, but it's not Hollywood – anyone can learn.

3
Sustaining and developing a freelance career

Congratulations! We'll assume you've made it and that you've joined the ranks of the freelances. Now there's a very important question to answer, 'What next?' It is quite possible that for a short time the answer will be 'Nothing'. Nothing that is, apart from acquiring experience and expertise and gradually becoming known, and hopefully respected, in the sector of the industry that you work in. Of course, this is far from *doing nothing* because you are part of one of the fastest-moving industries you're ever likely to find. Techniques and equipment, new technology and let's be honest, fashions, change so rapidly that keeping up with what's happening in your sector of the business can be quite a task in itself.

It's more than likely, though, that the drive, energy and determination which helped you to get started in the industry in the first place will be driving you forward. In other words, once you have established yourself, your ambition is likely to assert itself. Unlike permanent employment, however, for the freelance there's no formal career structure or promotions board that allows you to move up the ladder of your profession. Once again, as a freelance, you are thrown back on your own resources; you're required to work it all out for yourself. How exactly you might be able to do that in order to sustain and nurture your career, and then to develop it, are the twin subjects of this chapter.

SUSTAINING YOUR FREELANCE CAREER

We've already seen the speed with which changes take place in the audio-visual industry. Keeping up with change in all of its many facets is a major preoccupation of the freelance and it's not as easy as it sounds. What you really need to do is to stay in touch with the industry and with the sector in which you are engaged so that you know what is going on. This sounds quite easy but actually requires a certain amount of discipline especially when both the time and the money you have to spend on this part of your life will probably be strictly limited. These are some of the means you can use to stay in touch with industry developments and full contact details are available in Chapter 10.

- *Trade unions* can bring many benefits to members, but one of the major assets is the information they can make available in publications, and perhaps particularly on their websites. Membership of BECTU (or NUJ for those involved or interested in factual programming) is probably well worth considering for the wide range of membership benefits. Considering that the freelance life can be quite isolated, it may be worth choosing a union that has a good network of branches so that you can attend meetings and find out what colleagues are thinking and doing.

- *Societies and associations* can provide similar benefits but are often more closely focused on skills and crafts. One such is BKSTS (British Kinematograph Sound and Television Society). Perhaps to overcome the difficulties of its slightly archaic, *Sunday-best* name it refers to itself as The Moving Image Society which is a very good summary of what it does through the lectures, seminars and meetings it organises. Another example is the Guild of Television Cameramen, a UK-based but internationally aspiring group, though how many women camera operators it attracts might be difficult to predict!

- *Newspapers and journals* are an invaluable way of keeping in touch with industry issues and preoccupations. The *Guardian Media Section* does this splendidly for more general media-related issues, and most of the unions and Societies produce monthly or quarterly journals, magazines or newsletters. Subscriptions to *Broadcast* magazine or the *Radio* would also be well worth considering.

- *The Internet* – there are many sites dedicated to industry matters in the UK and not a few concerning themselves with freelance issues, amongst them www.tvfreelancers.org.uk and www.productionbase.co.uk. A search for *tv freelance* will bring up more sites of interest.

There is, of course, more to sustaining your career than keeping up with industry trends. Your networks and contacts need to be in good shape too. From a professional point of view, the groups, societies and publications mentioned above will help in this respect. You will also need to think constructively about developing your networks in other directions and to make sure that potential clients and employers are kept aware of what you are doing.

Thinking and planning ahead

This is probably one of the most difficult things for a freelance to achieve. If you are working long and hard on a project, it may be difficult or impossible to spend much time and energy in the pursuit of the next job. If you don't do this, then you may well find that the gaps between work are longer than you would wish and more than you can afford. Some freelances have found that diary services or agencies can help here. This gives you the advantage of someone who is always available to answer the telephone when you are too busy to do so, they can also help to organise your diary and to keep time aside for holidays and rest periods. It may also be possible for such services to invoice clients on your behalf. You will of course have to be prepared to pay for the service, but depending on your particular circumstances it may well be worthwhile considering. You will be able to locate a range of agencies on the Internet by searching for *tv crew hire*. Alternatively, the Skills for Media website also provides a listing.[13]

Market yourself – even if a diary service or agency is not for you, marketing yourself is an activity you probably can't afford to neglect. You may well be able to achieve good results simply by being organised and disciplined in your approach to work. A little time taken to set up a working database of clients and potential clients could be very useful. Mail shots can be sent out from time to time, and letting clients know what you've been up to may be a useful way of reminding them that you're there and available for work. A note of caution though; freelances have to be discreet. The media business can be very secretive at times, rightly so because ideas can make money. Remember this and ensure that clients are happy for you to talk about the projects you've been working on. You don't have to go into any great detail; even a list of programmes you've been working on can be impressive to potential customers.

Keep your professional CV up to date – it is a good idea to keep your CV regularly updated so that it's standing by and ready to give to anyone who's interested. It will mean that you can avoid the last-minute panic of trying to bring it up to date when it's asked for and may avoid your forgetting to add a vital and prestigious piece of information!

DEVELOPING YOUR FREELANCE CAREER

So far in this chapter we have been concerned with what you need to do in order to keep your freelance career on an even keel and to prevent your skills from becoming blunted and your expertise outdated. In other words, we're talking about the brisk paddling you need to do to keep relatively stable in the fast-flowing waters of the industry. If you want to move on, if you have ambitions then you will probably need to consider further training and possibly further qualifications. As a freelance you will probably have to make yourself available at short notice and this does not make organising your life easy. It makes organising courses and securing the time you need to complete them even more problematic. In addition most courses have to be paid for and it's going to be you who has to find the money.

Industry perspective

Training is a freelance preoccupation – and that's official. More than two-thirds of all freelances feel that they have specific training needs and most cite the reasons for this as keeping up to date and to develop new technology skills. This information is derived from Skillset's 2002 Freelance survey.[14] An interesting feature of the findings is that the number of freelances who feel that they need business training has fallen by half since 1993. In other research carried out by Skillset, employers have highlighted this as a major gap in skills. Although these employers might be talking more specifically about permanent employees, the acquisition of business skills is an important issue which freelances would do well to take very seriously. Perhaps unsurprisingly, the main subject areas in which freelances stated they needed training were camera, video, web design, post-production and new media. Freelances felt that there were significant barriers to training, the most important of these were said to be cost (60 per cent mentioned this), lack of information about courses (50 per cent) and loss of earnings whilst undergoing training (37 per cent).

It's worth noting that the survey also reveals that about half of all freelances had received training in the past year. Of those who had been in the industry for up to five years, 75 per cent were likely to have received training in the past twelve months compared with only 31 per cent of those who entered the industry thirty years earlier. Given the rapidity of change and technological innovation within the industry it should be a matter of concern to freelances that there seems to be a growing lack of interest in training the longer they have been in the industry.

It is perhaps not surprising that there is an inverse correlation between training and earning since we have already seen that the newest entrants to the industry are among the most likely to have received some kind of training in the last twelve months. However, of the highest-earning group (earning £76K or more), no less than 63 per cent had undergone training in the previous year, a statistic well worth pondering by anyone who remains unsure of the value of training as part of their career development. Finally it is interesting to note that 25 per cent of training was paid for by the freelances themselves, 15 per cent by employers and 41 per cent was delivered at no cost (this last figure possibly being a mix of courses delivered free of charge or those involving self-study). A basic internet search of training opportunities reveals a huge range of courses available and a not inconsiderable number of funding bodies willing to consider financial support to cover at least part of the cost. It is perhaps not unreasonable to conclude that such opportunities lie within the grasp of most freelances who appreciate the significance and value of such training in their careers.

Developing a specialisation

One way of standing out from the crowd is to consider specialising within a particular area of your sector. It is sometime possible to combine two skills to provide potential clients with a particular expertise. A good example of this is Keith Partridge, a cameraman with over sixteen years' experience in shooting for film and television. As a keen and qualified climber he is able to offer his services as a 'climbing cameraman' and worked on the acclaimed cinema documentary *Touching the Void*.

There are, of course, many other examples of developing specialisations which can give your career an edge over the competition and help to guarantee a supply of projects and assignments. It is important, however, to bear in mind that whatever specialisation you might choose, it's essential that your expertise is well founded, and that you are fully aware of and trained in all the health and safety aspects of what you are undertaking. A specialisation need not be as spectacular as that of Keith Partridge; an interest in a particular period of history, in architecture or wildlife, for example, might well set you off on developing your skills and keeping your services in demand.

Where to find training information

The Independent Production Training Fund collects funds raised by means of a levy (0.25 per cent) on independent productions in the UK. Although strictly speaking this is a voluntary contribution, the BBC, ITV companies, C4 and Five deduct the fee from all the programmes they commission. This money is distributed to industry training organisations and makes a substantial contribution to the provision of training within the industry.

A number of organisations run short courses to help freelances and others keep their skills up to date or to learn new skills. A camera operator might for example wish to learn how to operate Steadicam (a special camera stabilising piece of equipment) in order to enhance the skills and services he has on offer. There a number of ways in which you can explore the possibilities.

Trade union, association or group – is a good starting point. If you've chosen well, you may even find that the association to which you belong actually runs suitable courses. In any case, they are more than likely to keep up-to-date lists of available courses. The advantage of this is that you're more likely to be able to benefit from the feedback from those who have already participated in the training. In some cases you may not even have to be a paid-up member to access training courses, though you may well pay a premium on the fees if you are not.

Industry bodies – are another excellent source of information and sometimes funding. For example, Sgrin, the media agency for Wales, can offer some funding for courses through the Skills Wales Fund. Similarly, Scottish Screen has comprehensive information on courses and funding. A full list of such agencies can be found in the reference section.

National Film & Television School Short Courses – are well worth investigating. The list of courses is very comprehensive and many are suitable for freelances. Group size is small and an additional attraction is that freelance rates are generally offered at about 50 per cent of the full fee. Courses are available under a number of subject headings, namely: production, camera and lighting, sound and editing, writing and directing, digital post-production and art and design. Most of the courses offered run for two to three days depending on the subjects covered.

The Skillset/BFI Media and Multimedia Searchable Database – is as comprehensive a list as you could wish for. It claims to have a database of nearly 5,000 courses, so you should expect to find something suitable for your needs. It can be consulted at: www.bfi.org.uk/education/courses/mediacourses/.

To try it out, I looked at what might be available for those who wished to specialise in wigs for the film and television industry – the database came up with a commendable seven available courses!

Academic courses

After a while working as a freelance, it might be worth considering further academic courses in order to enhance your work with the services you can offer your clients. Clearly the degree to which this is useful will depend very much on the work you do and the sector you work in. AGCAS (Association of Graduate Careers Advisory Services) provide a useful directory of postgraduate diploma and degree courses.[15] It will however be very important for you to ensure that the course matches your requirements as closely as possible. If you are leaning more towards vocational courses, make sure, for example, that those who are to teach you have a good track record in the industry, or have strong links with it. You should not hesitate to ask difficult or awkward questions of those running courses; after all you'll be spending a great deal of time and probably quite a bit of money on this part of your education.

MANAGING EXPECTATIONS

One thing should be clear to the new and intending freelance and that is not to expect too much too soon. A successful freelance needs to become known to potential employers and to develop a reputation not only for skill but reliability. Such reputations are built with care and over a period of time. You will not find it easy at the outset to find work, and it will probably be even more difficult to move from job to job without interruption. This means that it is likely that you will experience periods without income or at least without income from your chosen career. It would be realistic to expect to have to fill in between media jobs with other paying work or by claiming unemployment benefit. This is not an ideal situation but realistically there is little alternative. From speaking to a number of freelances about the early days of their careers it would seem to be wise to allow yourself at least two years before you expect to be working full time, without interruption, in your chosen sector. In managing your expectations you should be realistic about the difficulties you will encounter, not simply in terms of finding work and sustaining a career, but in the isolation and loneliness that can be part of the life of a freelance.

Freelance perspective

When you are a freelance you never lose the feeling that you can't take anything for granted, but it gives you more of an edge.
                                                        Freelance cameraman

Being freelance at least allows me to do what I want some of the time.
                                                        Freelance researcher

Freelancing is difficult if you have a family. A regular job means it's easier to make child-care arrangements.

Developing ideas and pitching is usually working for nothing.
                                                Freelance scriptwriter/producer

You have to deal with being dropped when a production is finished. You have to show loyalty, but don't expect to receive it.

You get used to being left in the cutting-room when everyone's having Christmas dinner!
                                                        Freelance editor

[Training] is much harder, you have to pay for yourself and your time is taken up and there's the difficulty of turning work down.
                                                        Freelance researcher

You have to be careful of long hours and low pay. It can be disheartening when you don't know what to expect, but don't sell yourself short. Targeting the right company is essential.
                                                Freelance researcher/director

Some people refer to freelances as casual labour, they want to do the 9 to 5 and have a safety net, but to me doing what you want is more important than security, but you've got to be thick-skinned and take rejection.

I do a very varied job, from a music video in New York to a football match in Moscow – it's the luxury of not being in a rut!
                                                        Freelance cameraman

4
Freelancing in radio

Many people in the media and in television in particular have spent at least some of the earlier parts of their careers in radio. So, in some ways, working in radio can quite properly be seen as a training ground and starting point for a career in television or other sectors of the media. My own early experience in local radio gave me a professional grounding, skills and experience which were invaluable throughout the rest of my working life. To be frank, it's not a bad way to learn your craft. Working in a small radio station away from the glare of too much publicity has distinct advantages. There, you can experience triumphs and disasters without doing yourself, or more importantly anybody else, too much harm! One of the great benefits of work in radio is that, whatever you do, you are likely to be involved in a wide range of activities from planning and presentation to editing and recording live speech, music and maybe even large-scale outside broadcast events. The precise nature of the experience will naturally depend on the genre of radio station. But before the roars of disapproval become too loud, I should make one or two strong reservations about encouraging anyone to see radio as a mere training ground for greater things. To do so would be a travesty and a grave disservice both to radio as a medium and to those who work in it.

To work in radio is itself a privilege. It is part of the daily lives of the public in a way television could not be – a constant companion to millions with an intimacy that would be hard to emulate. To see radio as second-best or as less important is to display a worrying ignorance about a medium which is both influential and – at its best – magically imaginative. There is nothing wrong with seeing radio as a good entry point into a media career but care needs to be exercised. Radio people are generally devotees of their medium and will not take kindly to any suggestion of it being used simply as a stepping stone by those who have set their sights on *higher things*. Prepare also to be captured and captivated; radio has a way of ensnaring and entrancing those who come into contact with it. A short spell 'for the experience' may well turn into a lifetime career.

As we've already seen in the preceding chapter, an important part of the preparation for looking for work of any kind is to do the research and to find out as much as you can about how your chosen field works and how the industry is structured.

THE SHAPE OF THE INDUSTRY

Radio in the UK today is a rapidly changing and highly professional industry. Much of the radio audience tends to be rather conservative in its listening habits, fiercely loyal and rarely switching stations and even then only between a few selected wavelengths. For this reason, few are aware of the sheer diversity of the programmes and stations available. If you are intending to look for work in the radio sector then it makes sense to know as much as possible about the business of radio broadcasting as you can — its scope and variety are breathtaking. This is a good point therefore to take a look at the sweep and scale of radio in the United Kingdom. There are a number of ways in which the industry can usefully be analysed.

Ownership and control

Ownership is an important tool with which to analyse the radio industry in the UK. Most importantly it reveals the sources of funding and the finance behind the stations as well as the bodies that are responsible for regulating the content and standards to be observed by the broadcaster.

BBC radio is funded from the revenue generated by the television licence. Other radio stations are funded by revenues generated by the sale of on-air advertising.

The BBC is the biggest radio broadcaster in the UK; it is a public corporation, governed by Royal Charter with the particular remit to deliver public service broadcasting. The stated aim of the BBC networks is to *inform, educate and entertain*. At the time of writing (before the Royal Charter renewal of 2007) the BBC continues to regulate itself through the Board of Governors whose duty it is to safeguard the public interest, the journalistic and editorial integrity of the BBC. The BBC is responsible for a wide variety of output in radio and has five analogue broadcast networks.

Table 4.1 illustrates that, in addition to the five analogue networks, the BBC also provides a range of output exclusively on digital or cable platforms.

In addition to these networks BBC World Service is available on different platforms depending on location. It is available in all areas on DAB and satellite and on AM in certain areas of the UK. As its name suggests, the World Service is intended to be a representative voice of Britain across the world, and as such is the only one of the BBC's services to receive a grant direct from the government. All other BBC services are funded from the licence fee and from the BBC's own commercial operations. All BBC radio networks are available on the Internet.

Table 4.1 BBC radio

Available on all platforms	
BBC Radio 1	New music
BBC Radio 2	Popular music and culture with a diverse range of specialist music, features, documentaries, light entertainment and readings
BBC Radio 3	Classical, jazz, world, arts, drama
BBC Radio 4	Speech, current affairs, drama, comedy
BBC Radio 5 Live	Live news, live sport
BBC World Service	The voice of Britain, available in forty-three languages
BBC radio available on DAB/Digital Television/Internet only	
1Xtra	New black music
BBC Radio 5 Live Sports Extra	More live sport
BBC Six Music	New music
BBC 7	Comedy, children's programming and drama
BBC Asian Network	News, music and drama for the UK Asian communities
BBC regional/national stations	
Radio Scotland	
Radio Wales	
Radio Ulster	
Radio Cymru	
Radio Foyle	
Radio Nan Gaidheal	
Local radio stations in England	Twenty stations throughout the country

Commercial radio is the generic term applied to broadcasters whose income is derived from the sale of advertising. All radio broadcasters are required to be licenced by Ofcom who took over the responsibilities of the Radio Authority at the beginning of 2004. As the legal regulator, Ofcom not only awards licences but also acts to ensure that codes and standards of content and programming are adhered to. Ofcom describes its own remit in the following terms:

> *Ofcom's specific duties fall into six areas:*
> 1 *Ensuring the optimal use of the electro-magnetic spectrum.*
> 2 *Ensuring that a wide range of electronic communications services – including high speed data services – is available throughout the UK.*
> 3 *Ensuring a wide range of TV and radio services of high quality and wide appeal.*
> 4 *Maintaining plurality in the provision of broadcasting.*
> 5 *Applying adequate protection for audiences against offensive or harmful material.*
> 6 *Applying adequate protection for audiences against unfairness or the infringement of privacy.*[16]

There are a number of major players in ownership terms. The *Guardian Media Group* for example owns Real Radio and currently has three stations serving central Scotland, South Wales and Leeds under that brand as well as Jazz FM in London. Scottish Radio holdings owns many commercial radio stations in Scotland including Radio Clyde, Radio Forth and Radio Tay. Table 4.2 is intended as an illustration of the pattern of ownership of UK commercial radio. The list is not comprehensive, and sales and acquisitions of individual stations and holding companies will, of course, bring changes in the pattern of ownership.

Platform

Platform is the term used by the industry to describe the method of transmission of a broadcast, and applies both to television and radio. The proliferation of radio station licences over the past few decades means that platform is an increasingly useful way of finding your way round the stations that are broadcasting and which might therefore offer potential employment to the freelance.

Analogue broadcasting on radio frequencies is, of course, the way radio has traditionally been delivered since the days of Marconi. A (literally) *wireless* medium, its reach depends entirely on the wavelengths used to radiate the signals. FM (frequency modulation) has the highest quality but the shortest distance – usually line-of-sight. A rough count of FM licensee radio stations in the UK on the Ofcom website[19] indicated at least 222 stations currently broadcasting on this waveband. AM (amplitude modulation) comprises both medium- and long-wave broadcasts. Its reach can vary from a few miles to hundreds of miles and is subject to atmospheric interference. Ofcom has a listing of more than sixty AM stations currently licensed. Short wave can reach across continents but is of very variable

Table 4.2 Some major UK radio groups

CN Group Ltd	seven stations, inc. Citybeat Belfast
Capital Radio plc	twenty-six stations, inc. Capital Gold and Century FM
Chrysalis Radio	ten stations, inc. LBC and LBC News
EMAP Performance Network	twenty-five stations, inc. Hallam and Magic
GWR Group plc	forty-two stations, inc. Classic FM
Lincs FM plc	eight stations, inc. Lincs FM and Rutland Radio
SMG	three stations, inc. Virgin and Virgin Classic Rock
Scottish Radio Holdings plc	twenty-one stations, inc. Westsound and Clyde 1
The Local Radio Company plc	twenty-two stations, inc. Central FM and Minster FM
The Wireless Group plc	seventeen stations, inc. Imagine FM and Signal 1
Tindle Radio Limited	eight stations, inc. The Beach and Dream 100
UBC Media Group plc	twenty-one stations, inc. Classic Gold and Oneword
UKRD Group Ltd	thirteen stations, inc. County Sound and Star

Source: Ofcom[17]/MediaUK[18] websites.

quality and very prone to atmospheric interference. Short-wave broadcasts were much favoured propaganda devices during the Cold War and subject to *jamming* or artificial interference from governments hostile to the originators of such programming.

Cable delivery accounts for a relatively small number of licences, fifteen are listed on the Ofcom site.

Satellite radio stations abound with 107 being licensed at the time of writing. Generally these are accessed by the public through television satellite connections such as BSB (British Sky Broadcasting).

Digital stations are delivered by local multiplexes. These are licensed to provide a range of programmes which are accessed by the listener using a DAB (Digital Audio Broadcasting) radio. Each multiplex has agreements with programme providers to carry both nationally and locally or regionally produced programming.

At this stage in the development of digital services it's perhaps tempting to think of digital, cable, satellite and Internet services as merely alternative ways of delivering a particular radio station to its audience. In many ways this is, of course, true. The BBC can, for example, make Radio 4 available in a variety of ways:

- FM;

- AM (in this case the old *long-wave*);

- DAB (Digital Audio Broadcasting);

- Satellite Broadcasting (by the Sky Network, for example);

- Cable distribution (by NTL for example);

- On the Internet (via the BBC website in this case).

It soon becomes apparent, however, that these alternative modes of delivery or platforms offer far more than a simple choice of ways to tune-in. New audiences are targeted and reached by these methods. The Internet can make it possible to *broadcast* a radio network anywhere in the world where an Internet connection is possible. Paradoxically it can also aid *narrowcasting* in that it makes programming both possible and practical at relatively low cost to small common-interest groups.

Genre

Genre may be the single most important criterion for a person seeking work in the radio sector. A deep interest in highly crafted speech programmes like dramas, features and documentaries is unlikely to be fulfilled in a radio station devoted almost exclusively to Top 40 chart shows. This is not to suggest, of course, that the freelance will always have the luxury of working on programmes which deeply appeal to individual personal tastes – that would indeed be a luxury. It is however going to be a distinct advantage in gaining work if the potential freelance can demonstrate at least some knowledge, enthusiasm or sympathy with the content of the programme or the genre of the station. A glance at practically any reasonably comprehensive listing of radio stations will reveal an astonishing range of station identities and genres from the talking books of Oneword (a digital and satellite service) to specialist radio stations in London for both Greek and Turkish communities, for example.

Geographical reach

A further way of considering the radio industry is to think of broadcasting in terms of geographical reach. Clearly the presence of any radio station on the Internet ensures a virtual world-wide reach. It is nevertheless meaningful to classify radio stations according to the geographical area they seek to service. Local radio stations will serve particular cities, towns or rural communities based on small towns. Such stations may be part of the BBC's network of local radio stations. Alternatively, commercial stations serving similar geographical areas may be entirely independent or, as is increasingly the case, part of a group of stations owned by a large commercial enterprise. In many ways, the geographical spread and local roots of these stations offer many opportunities to the enterprising freelance. The geographical reach of a radio station can also be a critical factor in the choices to be made by the freelance. There is a difference between network (UK-wide) radio and local or regional broadcasting, and network is not necessarily better than local, though it certainly is different. It's true that, generally speaking, the bigger the audience, the bigger the programme budget will be. However, many of those working in the radio industry value very highly the local or regional roots of a broadcaster and the commitment that such a base makes possible to an identifiable local community. Much the same argument can also be advanced for more specialist radio stations, though this time they appeal to a community of interest, in say, the ethnic background or the particular musical tastes of the audience. It's worth bearing in mind the personal preferences and intended career path of the freelance. Would a particular individual be happier as a relatively small cog in a large machine or as a larger cog in a smaller machine? It's a vitally important question, the answer to which may have a significant impact on the happiness and personal fulfilment of the freelance. A London-based, metropolitan-centred career should not be an automatic choice, nor should an inexorable rise through management (which usually does entail at least a significant spell in the capital). In any case, a freelance career is perhaps not the best way of pursuing such management ambitions, at least not in the long term.

Companies are likely to look for significant experience within a company setting from those they are going to promote to senior positions.

WHAT JOBS ARE AVAILABLE

If nothing else, the preceding paragraphs in this chapter will have indicated the huge range and variety of radio stations now available to the listener throughout the UK. This suggests an equally huge range of work opportunities for the freelance. A word of caution, however; a proliferation of stations does not necessarily bring a proliferation of opportunities for the freelance worker. All radio stations are now able to take advantage of computerised planning and play-out facilities, and may owe their existence to the possibility of low cost, automated procedures, thus reducing the need for high staff levels and, consequently, high wage bills. Paradoxically this may give the freelance a competitive edge over those seeking permanent contracts of employment. The freelance is able to offer hours or days of work and is not necessarily seeking a long-term or intensive financial commitment from the radio station. This may well be a very attractive proposition to a smaller broadcaster. The aspiring freelance does need to be enterprising, however, because a certain amount of ingenuity and determination is required to track down the contact information of the various operators in the geographical area that is of interest. The BBC and major commercial groups are more easily researched and have clear and informative websites, often with helpful guidance as to how to find work. More specialised stations may be less easy to track down, especially if you are not aware of their existence in the first place! A useful stopping off point here is the Ofcom website which maintains up-to-date listings of all licensed stations in operation. For digital stations, the Ofcom site lists all digital multiplex licensees and, where possible, provides web links to these operators who then list the stations they carry on their own multiplexes.

There are a number of areas within radio broadcasting that offer the potential of work to the freelance. The Radio Academy, a professional body for people within the radio industry, has produced a CD, *Getting into Radio.* This is available to listen to or download as mp3 files on the Academy website. The files contain advice and information from those working in radio. They cover a range of occupations including engineering, production, sales and marketing, journalism, commercial production and presentation. The Academy also publishes a quarterly newsletter, and is perhaps best known as the originator of the prestigious Sony Radio Academy Awards. Details of how to contact the academy are given in the reference section.

Production

Producers have authority, and therefore responsibility, for the programme-making process. The precise scope and limits of such authority will vary from company to company but will usually require the exercise of editorial judgment in terms of programme content, possibly choosing or at least looking after the talent engaged to take part in the programme. Generally, producers are also responsible for negotiating budgets and for sticking to them! Depending on the kind of programming, the producer may well have to take the programme through its post-production phase and make sure that it runs to time. There are no formal qualifications for radio producers, although of course many colleges and universities run radio production courses. Experience is highly prized and, again, certain types of programming will value experience in a particular field. A consumer programme might well benefit from a producer with a legal, public affairs or journalism background. Similarly, specialist music programmes will probably be run by people with considerable knowledge of this field. It's worth bearing in mind too that not all production functions are carried out by producers – assistant producers and researchers often have a large part to play, and may well record and edit individual items or packages which make up the programme. Much of the detail of how the production of a particular programme is managed will depend on the broadcaster concerned and on the genre of the programming.

Journalism

Radio stations require journalists to have skills in newsgathering, news writing and presentation. Technical competence will also be needed as increasingly journalists are required not only to record but to edit their material for broadcast. Formal qualifications are not necessarily required, but these will be quite useful and may be specified by some employers. Courses are available at Further Education level from many colleges. In the higher education sector, many universities run journalism courses at both undergraduate and postgraduate level. For further information on education and training for broadcast journalism it's worth consulting the Broadcast Journalism Training Council.[20] Local commercial stations and, of course, BBC News employ journalists, but there are also major specialised news providers in the commercial context, and it is certainly worthwhile contacting them for the prospect of freelance work. IRN (Independent Radio News) is a division of ITN. It supplies news to many commercial radio stations, as does Global Radio News. Contact details for both are found in the reference section.

Commercial production

This refers to the production of commercials to be used by advertisers in radio programmes. Most, if not all, radio stations have a commercial production section to enable commercials for local advertisers to be produced cost effectively. Major advertisers of an international or national nature tend to use advertising agencies and production facility houses to make their commercials. Working in commercial production can be a very good first step in finding work in a radio station. This department is usually quite busy and may also experience seasonal pressure and the consequent need to take on additional staff on a short-term basis. Working in a commercial production department gives a freelance worker an opportunity to observe the radio station at close quarters. Whilst there is the pressure to produce high-quality and accurate work to a set budget, the department is insulated to a great extent from the pressures and stress of live broadcasting – an ideal place to find one's strengths and weaknesses.

Presentation

This is what's known as the *talent* end of the business – most presenters are freelance and are employed on fixed-term contracts. Mapping a career structure for a freelance presenter is not an easy task. Most who present radio programmes have long nurtured a burning ambition to do so and would find it difficult to imagine doing anything else. Others have wandered into presentation almost by accident perhaps having worked in production, journalism or even acting. Those outside the radio industry are often surprised by the number of radio presenters who have gained their first experience as presenters in hospital radio. Many hospital radio stations have developed highly competent training schemes and teach studio skills and disciplines as well as presentation skills with a large element of success. The Hospital Broadcasting Association can provide information about participating groups throughout the UK.[21]

Student radio stations can and often do fulfil similar functions and provide invaluable pre-professional experience and training.[22] Determination and resilience are probably key qualities to nurture in the intending freelance presenter and the experience gained in simply being in the radio station giving general assistance where it's required will be invaluable.

Engineering

If you are interested in the technical or engineering side of radio, then engineering or electronics qualifications at college or university level are obviously going to be very helpful. It is worth remembering, however, that as in all other sectors of work in the audio-visual industry, routes into employment can be varied. It may well be that gaining experience in a local station will provide you with a very good start. As in most media jobs, you will have to be prepared to do the menial tasks and to run around for people who have a lot more experience than you. Those who work in engineering stress that what is required is a mixture of elements:

- experience;

- training;

- the ability to communicate;

- the ability to work as a member of a small team;

- the ability to work under pressure (especially when things go wrong!).

The range of jobs grouped under the umbrella of engineering in radio is massive, from research and development, through work on transmitters, studio design and equipment maintenance to working directly with audio as a sound designer or studio operator. You should also remember that, with broadcasters such as the BBC, engineers, especially outside London, may be required to work across both radio and television. They may in these circumstances be described as *broadcast engineers*. This will be seen as an advantage to some, but will be less attractive to those who would prefer to specialise in either radio or television. If you would like to find out more about the work of engineers in the audio-visual industry, then you could visit the BBC website which gives details of graduate recruitment schemes and also provides case studies of engineers who work for the corporation. Manx Radio also provides a useful case study, simply because it operates in such a small community that it has to provide all the engineering services a radio station requires. The website at www.manxradio.com/engineering gives an excellent thumbnail sketch with photographs of the work of the radio engineering department.

Once again, those working in the industry emphasise the part that hospital radio and RSL stations (Restricted Radio Licences) can play in providing experience. Often, experience gained in working in such stations may lead on to college or university courses, so it's by no means necessary to start with courses of study. As always, flexibility is the key, as is the ability to make full use of the experience and the contacts such work provides.

Industry perspective

It's reported by Skillset (2003) that about 28 per cent of jobs in the broadcast radio sector are carried out by freelance or short-term contract staff, and a further 4 per cent is added if sole traders are included. There also appears to be a healthy market for freelances in the engineering and studio operations sectors at 13 per cent and 14 per cent respectively, though here both television and radio are combined. The Department for Education and Skills carries out Skills dialogues and investigations across various industries. It notes that:

> *broadcasters report difficulties recruiting broadcast engineers.*
> Media and Creative Industries Skills Dialogue

5
Freelancing in television

There is a Chinese curse which says, 'May he live in interesting times.' Like it or not, we live in interesting times . . .
Robert F. Kennedy in a speech in Cape Town, South Africa, 7 June 1966

THE SHAPE OF THE INDUSTRY

Television in the UK is dominated by three major broadcasters, the BBC, ITV and BSkyB. Of these, the largest in revenue terms is the satellite broadcaster BSkyB. This is an industry which is subject to a relatively rapid rate of change. At the time of writing, the BBC is preparing for the renewal of its charter at the end of 2006 and the ITV network is moving from a federal structure of many independent companies towards a single, global company. Satellite broadcasting has, over the past decade, moved from a subsidiary player to one of immense significance – at least in commercial terms. In addition, the government is actively pursuing a policy of moving away from analogue delivery of television services to an all-digital system with a target date of 2010 for what is described as *analogue switch-off*. The BBC is charged with a responsibility for Public Service Broadcasting (PSB) though it is not, of course, the sole provider of such programming. The ITV network is obliged under the terms of its licences to provide a minimum number of programming hours across a wide range of genres, many of which, such as coverage of the arts, religion or local news and current affairs programmes, are unquestionably of a public service nature. There is, however, no clear definition of what public service broadcasting actually is, let alone a legal definition. It is generally agreed to revolve around the provision of high quality, diverse programming for a range of interests and audiences, with an agenda that is not constrained by commercial pressures or the demands for consistently high ratings success. The rather unsatisfactory definition of PSB raises as many questions as it answers. The huge increase in competition brought about by the proliferation of broadcast outlets has put ITV under great commercial pressure so that the regulator OFCOM is considering relaxing some of the public service obligations of the network when the licences are renewed in 2006. Such commercial pressures, together with the absence of a satisfactory definition of public service broadcasting have led to a major review. The Communication Act required OFCOM to carry out a review of public service broadcasting and to provide recommendations for maintaining and strengthening the quality of PSB television.

These are the *interesting times* in which the television freelance operates and to which the new entrant aspires.

As with the radio industry, there are a number of useful ways in which the structure of the industry can be described.

OWNERSHIP AND CONTROL

The BBC – all of the BBC's activities including television, radio, interactive and commercial operations are the responsibility of the board of governors of the BBC. They in turn operate under the Corporation's Royal Charter, due for renewal at the end of 2006. The BBC is its own regulator in that the governors take ultimate responsibility for editorial policy, content, and for taste and decency issues. In this sense the BBC regulates itself without reference to outside agencies. The Hutton report in 2004 made a number of damaging criticisms of the BBC's control of editorial policy and led directly to the resignations of both the Chairman of the Governors and the Director General of the corporation. This was as a result of Andrew Gilligan's report on the Radio 4 *Today* programme about the government's handling of intelligence material concerning weapons of mass destruction in Iraq. It remains to be seen whether, in the light of this damaging controversy, the BBC is permitted to retain quite the same degree of autonomy that it has previously enjoyed or whether it will be subject to some external regulation.

Ofcom – apart from the BBC and S4C, all television broadcasting – analogue, terrestrial digital, satellite or cable – is licensed and regulated by Ofcom. In the case of all broadcasters, including the BBC and S4C, the regulator has the authority

- to direct that a programme not be repeated;
- to direct that a correction or a statement of Ofcom's findings be broadcast;
- to impose a fine (to a maximum of £250,000 on the BBC and S4C).

With the exception of the BBC, Channel 4 or S4C, Ofcom has the power in an extreme case to shorten or even to revoke a broadcaster's licence. Nevertheless, part of the intention of the legislation[23] which created Ofcom was to deregulate and to take a lighter touch in its approach to carrying out its duties than some of the bodies whose work it had inherited. Under the Communications Act, 2003, Ofcom has a duty to:

- balance the promotion of choice and competition with the duty to foster plurality, informed citizenship, protect viewers, listeners and customers, and promote cultural diversity.

- serve the interests of the citizen-consumer as the communications industry enters the digital age.

- support the need for innovators, creators and investors to flourish within markets driven by full and fair competition between all providers.

- encourage the evolution of electronic media and communications networks to the greater benefit of all who live in the United Kingdom.

ITV – as suggested earlier, the ITV network has been changing through a series of mergers and acquisitions. Its structure was essentially federal with a number of independent companies like Granada and HTV, for example, providing content for their own regions and, in addition, contributing programming for the entire network. As a result of legislation relaxing rules on media ownership, the merger of Carlton and Granada was accomplished with the approval of the Secretary of State in early 2004. The ownership of twelve of the fifteen regional licences is now in the hands of one company, ITV plc. At present, the licences for Grampian and Scottish (owned by SMG plc), Channel and Ulster are outside the ownership of ITV plc. How long this will continue to be the case remains to be seen. It should also be noted that two licences remain outside the strictly regional nature of the ITV network. These are TVAM and ITN.

TVAM holds the licence to broadcast throughout the UK at breakfast time from 6 am to 9.25 am and under the terms of its licence is committed to the provision of a broad range of programming including news and current affairs. The company has also committed itself to regional content opt-outs (provided by regional broadcasters), for news, weather and travel and a regional representation within the main body of its programming.

ITN (Independent Television News) provides news programming for the ITV network and Channel 4. The organisation also provided news for Five (formerly *Channel Five*) until January 2005 when Five awarded its contract for the provision of news bulletins to Sky News. It should also be noted that ITN provides a broad range of other news-related services. These include the production of radio news for a large number of commercial radio stations under the banner of IRN (Independent Radio News).

Channel 4 – established in 1982, a publicly-owned corporation, with a board appointed by Ofcom (inheriting the roles and responsibilities of the former regulator, the Independent Television Commission or ITC). According to the Communication Act of 2003 its particular remit is to:

- demonstrate innovation, experimentation and creativity;

- appeal to the tastes and interests of a culturally diverse society;

- include programmes of an educational nature;

- exhibit a distinctive character.

Of particular interest to the freelance is that Channel 4 does not produce its own programmes; all its output is commissioned or bought in from sources outside the corporation. In that sense Channel 4 has been the single major contributor to the rise of the independent production sector in the UK.

Five – the latest, and presumably the last of the terrestrial stations to be licensed started broadcasting in 1997. After a rather interesting start as Channel 5 (initially attracting its audience with late evening *adult* content) it is now rebranded as *Five* and is gaining a reputation for new approaches to arts, history and factual programming. Five generates freelance employment because its programmes are commissioned externally, mainly from independent producers and are not made in house.

S4C (Channel 4 Wales) – on air since 1982, despite its title, S4C is not Channel 4 in Wales, though it does re-broadcast much of C4's programming, although programmes are generally rescheduled. It has a statutory obligation to broadcast in the Welsh language at peak times, and has a second digital channel S4C 2 which is primarily concerned with coverage of the National Assembly for Wales. The station is funded directly by treasury grant, supplemented by the sale of its own advertising. Most significantly, S4C commissions all its programmes from independent producers and HTV and therefore indirectly provides a significant amount of work for freelances in Wales.

BSkyB (British Sky Broadcasting) – Sky's first programmes were downloaded to British homes for the first time in 1989 from the Astra satellite. Eighteen months later around one million homes were connected. Aggressive programming, marketing and rights acquisitions, especially in sports meant that by the mid-1990s satellite and cable accounted for a 10.8 per cent share of the UK viewing audience. By the end of 2003, Sky had seven million subscribers.

INDEPENDENT PRODUCTION – THE INDIES

Those unfamiliar with the intricacies of the broadcast television industry might be forgiven for being confused by the term *independent*, for there are independent television companies and independent production companies. Having now contributed to the confusion, I should explain. Independent Television (known also as ITV) is made up of a number of *independent* companies which formed a federation to provide programming for Channel 3. Such companies form what should perhaps be better known as Commercial Television, funded by advertising revenue rather than by the licence fee. This federal structure is now rapidly becoming a unitary structure (see ITV, p. 56).

Independent production companies (*indies*) on the other hand are by definition producers and not broadcasters. The definition is enshrined in law by the Broadcasting (Independent Productions) order of 1991 and subsequent amendments. This law ensures that, to be defined as an independent production company, no broadcaster may own more than 25 per cent of that company. There are limits too on how much an *indie* may own of a broadcaster. The reason for these legal definitions is that the market for independent production is protected and that broadcasters like the BBC and ITV are legally obliged to commission 25 per cent of their programming from the independent sector.

The quota applies to:

- Channel 3;
- Channel 4;
- Channel 5;
- BBC.

Production outside London

The Channel 4 licence specifies that 30 per cent of production spending should be outside London. ITV has committed to a non-metropolitan target spend of 50 per cent. The BBC has committed itself to a 33 per cent spend outside the South East of England. There are also genre-specific commitments within this to programming for the network from Scotland, Wales and Northern Ireland.

Codes of practice

Misgivings about the unequal power relationship between major broadcasters and smaller independent production companies led to legislation within the Communication Act of 2003. This gave Ofcom the duty to require broadcasters to establish codes of practice to cover their commercial dealings with independents in terms of reasonable timescales for the commissioning of programmes, and more particularly the ownership of various rights in formats and productions. This question of commercial rights had long been a bone of contention between independent producers and broadcasters, with the indies complaining that broadcasters retained too large a proportion of the rights to exploitation of programmes and formats.

The motivation for legislation and regulation in what is known as the Programme Supply Market was to:

- Strengthen the longer-term viability and growth potential of the independent production sector;

- Safeguard original UK production against the background of the Government's proposed changes to media ownership rules;

- Support production in the Nations and Regions; and

- Strengthen commitment to training across the sector.

ITC Press Release November 2002

Industry perspective

Independent producers are hugely important as providers of work for freelances and in many ways are responsible for the growth and viability of freelance employment. Skillset figures (2002) estimate that just over half the workforce in the independent sector is freelance and that 13 per cent of all freelances work for indies compared with 10 per cent working for TV broadcasters and 11 per cent working for radio broadcasters.

COMMERCIAL PRODUCTION

This sector refers to the production of commercials for television. It is part of the industry which relies heavily on the freelance workforce. The latest survey results indicate that, taken together, freelances and sole traders account for nearly 70 per cent of the workers in the sector.[24] The sector has rather more affinity with the world of film production than it does with broadcast television, and the crossover between crew members working in commercials and in film appears to be higher than between commercial production and television production. This seems to apply across all occupational groups within the sector, although there is little direct evidence to confirm or deny the validity of this impression. In other words, commercial production seems to be a specialisation, and an important one in the freelance world.

Industry perspective

Commercial production is the biggest single provider of freelance work in the audio-visual industry. It accounts for 20 per cent of all freelance employment, and within the sector, 80 per cent of work is carried out by freelances.[25]

WHAT JOBS ARE AVAILABLE

Freelance jobs are available across an enormous number of occupational groups within the sectors which form the television business. They range from work in production and post-production to make-up and hairdressing. What you really need to know, however, is which sectors traditionally recruit significant numbers of freelance workers for their projects. Table 5.1, adapted from data published by Skillset, shows these sectors ranked according to the proportion of freelances they employ.

The table gives an interesting insight into those occupational groups which are more likely to offer opportunities for freelance work, though it should be remembered that the table only indicates the percentage of freelances within the sector and is not an indication of the size of the sector itself. However, the table gives a very useful reminder of the sheer diversity of occupations within the industry and especially in what might broadly be called 'television', as opposed to the more narrowly defined 'television sector'. Although it is not within the scope of this book to give a detailed outline of each occupation, such career guides are available and some of them are listed in the reference section in Chapter 10. It is, however, worth looking at the principal groupings of occupations within television. These too are deceptively simple and contain many strands which offer opportunities to the freelance.

Table 5.1 Type of contract by occupational group

Sector	Permanent (%)	Freelance (%)
Make-up and hairdressing	10	90
Lighting	17	83
Special physical effects	30	70
Runner	36	64
Producing	51	49
Camera	53	47
Costume and wardrobe	56	44
Animation	62	38
Production	65	35
Radio broadcasting	66	34
Art and design	82	18
Journalism and sport	84	16
Interactive media	84	16
Other	85	15
Studio operations	86	14
Post-production	86	14
Broadcast engineering	87	13
Library and archives	90	10
Sound	93	7
Television broadcasting	94	6
Transmission	95	5
Programme distribution	96	4

Source: Skillset Workforce Survey 2003.

Production

It is easy but misguided to think only of producing and directing within the production area. In many ways, of course, these are the key jobs, and it may be worth spending a moment defining these two occupations, as they often cause some confusion amongst those not too familiar with the production process.

The producer – is the person who is editorially responsible for the programme, from its conception to its delivery to the commissioner. Producers are answerable to senior producers, editors and executive producers. The bigger the programme in terms of prestige, network slot, perceived importance and budgetary spend, the more complex will be these layers of management. The producer has the responsibility of ensuring that budgets are adhered to and that, editorially, the programme meets its requirements in terms of content, quality and technical standards. The producer may well be the creative driving force behind the whole project and will often have had the decisive say in who is hired for the production team. In these cases, the producer may be responsible not as much for creative input but for making sure that a long-running series is kept not only fresh, but loyal to its format.

The director – in simplified terms the director is responsible for *putting the pictures on the programme*. This is an oversimplified explanation but it does go to the heart of the director's job. As a director you take responsibility for the look, style and, of course, the sound of the programme. Again, depending on the genre of the programme, this role could be by far the most important. In drama, for example, the director's stamp is perhaps the defining creative contribution. In other programmes, the director's job will be primarily concerned with ensuring that the crew covers the required amount of work in each *shooting day* and that the shots gathered will ultimately be what the editor needs to shape the programme into its recognised format so that it fits with the rest of the series (some of which may well have been produced by other crews). It is the director's job to direct! As director you work closely with the camera operator to choose the type of shots and angles you need. You ensure that the sound recordist is generally happy with the sound obtained and you work closely with the talent, monitoring and guiding the performance and style of actors and presenters. In the post-production phase, the director can expect to be heavily committed to the editing process and may well log (or make a list of) the recorded material and, along with the editor, decide how best to assemble the material to make the programme according to specification.

The researcher – is a key role in the production process especially in factual programmes. In other genres similar and related roles may be played by members of the production team with specialist knowledge. A drama or drama series may have a location manager or location researcher who, as the name implies, has a very important role in finding suitable locations for filming and recording to take place, obtaining permissions and access. In much of the rest of television production, the researcher plays an equally vital part in the programme-making process. In factual programmes and series, it is generally the job of the researcher to find people to take part. If you've watched programmes showing how series like *Big Brother* are made, you'll be aware of how important researchers are in sifting through the thousands of applications received from people who want to take part.

The work of the researcher is of particular importance to those considering a career in television, freelance or otherwise. It is a key entry point into the business for many graduates. One of the main reasons for this is the flexibility the job may offer in terms of opportunities. The vital requirements are imagination, hard work, diligence and reliability. Quite often, specialised television skills are lower down the list of priorities. College or university experience of working together will (or should have) instilled the basics of how a crew goes about its work, when to keep quiet and what the vocabulary of the industry means. For many junior research jobs, this basic knowledge is sufficient to get started. From this point, the quality of the researcher's work will speak for itself. If you are a researcher, the producer or director to whom you answer will be interested in how reliable you are, how reliable is the information you provide and how your judgment of other people can be rated. As the researcher gains experience and some seniority, opportunities may well arise to make significant contributions in more specialised areas such as camera and directing.

In many ways the researcher is the first of the roles which can be combined with other roles or skills in portfolio jobs which seem to be increasingly popular in the audio-visual industry. Thus you may discover:

- the researcher/director;

- the senior researcher/director;

- the researcher/cameraman or camerawoman;

- the self-shooting director (not a director with a death wish but one who on occasion will shoot footage for the programme!).

And, of course,

- the producer/director.

Whilst this proliferation of jobs and titles may be amusing, or even bemusing, it illustrates not only the flexibility which may be required within the occupational group, but also, on a more positive note, it underlines the opportunities which exist to gain knowledge and experience from others in the production team. This expertise can then be used in support of efforts to apply for increasingly senior work.

The runner – is without doubt the entry point favoured by many looking for a first taste of paid work in the industry. The nature of the work done by the runner varies from project to project, but generally involves being available for a variety of relatively menial tasks, the most famous of which are making tea and coffee for the crew and talent, and finding sandwiches for the director! More serious work will entail making sure that tapes and rushes are delivered to their final destinations, and making travel arrangements. Depending on the size of the production, the runner may well have to buy consumables for a shoot, and hold a certain amount of petty cash. The work of the runner is very much what you make of it, and it does give individuals in their first professional role the ability to shine as reliable, enthusiastic and full of initiative. Probably the main incentive for the runner is not to stay a runner, but to quickly move on to positions with more responsibility and creativity. The importance of the role for the novice freelance probably lies in the unparalleled experience it gives of how the industry operates and the contacts that can be made whilst carrying out small but important jobs in the day-to-day life of a production.

Craft or technical roles

There are a number of roles in television production in which freelances are frequently to be found. The roles of camera operator, sound recordist and editor differ from those in production, because they deal only with a certain part of the production process, although that part may be extremely important. It would be wrong to think of these as simply technical operations because they may well involve a high degree of creativity and make a major contribution to the success or otherwise of the project.

Camera operator – is a rather unsatisfactory term because, in the film industry, this role has a particular connotation; strictly speaking a camera operator is the person who literally sets the camera in position, ensures that it is level, is loaded with film and ready for use. The operator may well switch it on and off when directed. It is the role of the cameraman to place the camera, fine tune the lighting and set the correct exposure. In modern production, because *cameraman* is seen as a sexist term, and the use of *cameraman* and *camerawoman* seems a little clumsy, *camera operator* has become the more acceptable job signifier. The camera operator may work in a studio or on location and use film, or more commonly electronic video equipment. Camera operators do not tend to require specific qualifications; experience and ability are more important, as are good coordination and what is known as 'a good eye', a mysterious phrase which is concerned with the ability to frame a good shot and an instant ability to know how to film a sequence so that the shots will make sense when they are edited. Nevertheless, courses may help enormously with an understanding of the technical and technological issues in film or video photography. Highly qualified and experienced camera operators may well take work requiring a very high degree of technical skill and creativity where their input artistically is on an equal footing with that of the director. In such circumstances they may well be engaged and credited for *photography* (never photographer) or as director of photography.

Camera assistant – it would be unusual for a relatively inexperienced freelance to be offered work as a camera operator except in the simplest of projects where budgets are very restricted. The role of the camera assistant is largely self-explanatory and involves helping the camera operator, often by carrying the tripod for many miles on location and by setting up and levelling the camera as instructed. Again this role is good for the learning experience it provides and for the opportunities that may arise for the assistant to shoot some sequences.

Sound recordist – is often the unsung hero or heroine of the production crew. Sadly, sound may be taken for granted by other members of a production crew yet its quality can greatly enhance a sequence. Similarly, poor sound can ruin a shoot and make the footage, however good, virtually unusable. Like the camera operator, experience and ability are of more importance than formal qualifications, though many courses are available which teach basic and advanced recording techniques and technology.

Sound assistant – again it would be unusual for an inexperienced freelance to obtain work without first having worked as an assistant. The role provides a very good opportunity to gain the experience and confidence required of a sound recordist.

Videotape or film editor – editors play a vital role in the post-production phase of a project. The work of editor involves sequencing the filmed material so that it makes sense both artistically and logically. It may mean working largely unsupervised by the director who provides notes and shot lists. On the other hand some directors will want to be very involved in the editing process, so editors have to be fairly flexible in the way they work. Not only do editors require a practised eye, and an intuitive knowledge of what will work when piecing together a sequence, video editors also need an intimate knowledge of the computer software commonly used in editing.

Other skilled technical and craft roles – of a more specialised nature are also often carried out sometimes almost exclusively by freelances or by the self-employed. These include lighting and electrician, make-up, costume and wardrobe, prompt (often known as autocue) operators, for example.

Engineering

Engineering work within the audio-visual industry covers a very wide range of activity and specialisation from the design and maintenance of transmitters, for example, to running complex studios or maintaining equipment in good order.

Job titles and descriptions vary from employer to employer. Variations will also occur depending on the location and scale of the facilities concerned. Outside of London, for example, it is more likely that an engineer will require a wide range of skills and a diversity of experience. Specialisation is more likely in larger concentrations of broadcasting activity in London and the South East. Qualifications at certificate, diploma or degree level may be required for entry to some jobs, and some employers, especially the BBC, offer traineeships from time to time. It is only fair to point out that many of the engineering roles in broadcasting are not traditionally ones where freelances are commonly found. This may well be because of the need to have a detailed knowledge of the practices, equipment and policy of the individual employer, and the certification requirements of some procedures with important health and safety implications. If you are interested in developing a freelance career in this sector of the industry, the best advice would be to seek information from employers and organisations like Skillset or FT2 as early as possible. It may also be worth considering a period of permanent employment with an established broadcaster in order to gain the necessary experience before establishing a freelance presence.

Journalism

Freelance journalists play an important role in the audio-visual industry. It is perhaps too easy to see the journalist only in the role of reporter. This is understandable because news gathering is such an important and highly visible function in broadcast radio and television. Yet journalists are to be found in many other roles too. In production and editorial roles in factual programmes, for example, a journalistic training or background can provide an excellent range of highly sought after skills. Because journalism is a large and complex activity with its own trade union, codes of practice and working methods, a consideration of freelance opportunities for journalists falls outside the scope of this book. It is, however, fully covered in a companion volume in this series.

6

Freelancing in non-broadcast

Non-broadcast work is a very important and sometimes underestimated part of the audio-visual industries in the UK. Whilst freelancing in the media is often understood to mean working in print, radio or television, a significant part of the industry undertakes work which is never intended for publication, heard on the radio or seen on television channels. There are a number of sectors which make up this division of the industry. Table 6.1 below provides an indication of the range of activities, the numbers of workers involved and the percentage of freelances within these groups.

It might at first glance seem rather strange to include facilities, hire and post-production as part of non-broadcast as many of the activities they carry out may well be services provided to broadcast productions. Clearly there is no neat solution to this dilemma; they have been included here because they are not directly concerned with the supply of programmes to the broadcast media.

The figures in Table 6.1 provide an interesting insight into the relative strength of what might broadly be described as *new media* activity compared with the more traditional field of corporate production. It is also interesting to note how the pro-

Table 6.1 Freelances in non-broadcast work

Sector	Total	Freelance (%)
Corporate production	2,800	43
Facilities	8,000	17
Studio/equipment hire	2,900	20
Post production	4,800	13
Interactive media	51,800	19
Online	34,900	24
Computer games	7,900	5
CD-ROM and other	9,000	11

Source: Skillset Census 2003.

portion of freelance workers drops quite markedly outside the traditional production sectors. One explanation for this might well be that certain activities like the development of computer games may have long development phases compared with video production and are therefore less suitable for freelance employment patterns. In addition, the contribution of individual key members within such a development team may well be more crucial so that there is an added incentive to offer long-term employment to such key members. Despite the somewhat variable attraction of these sectors in terms of freelance employment, the table does indicate the relatively high numbers engaged in such work. It may well be that a new entrant to the freelance market would do well to explore the opportunities that employment in the non-broadcast sector might offer. It is outside the scope of this book to deal with the computer games sector – it has its own special skills and requirements. It would be wrong, however, to overlook the opportunities that may nevertheless present themselves to a freelance with skills in audio or video techniques. Equally, realism suggests that, because only 5 per cent of workers engaged in developing and producing computer games are freelance, this sector is unlikely to prove a very fruitful source of freelance employment.

CORPORATE PRODUCTION

This sector is a lively and important part of the audio-visual industry and yet is often overlooked, perhaps especially by those embarking on their careers. This may happen because, on the whole, corporate production is undertaken by small and medium-sized enterprises (SMEs) operating quietly and less visibly than those working in the broadcast field. Corporate production is focused on serving the needs of business and commerce in a variety of ways. Programmes are usually fairly short, at around four to ten minutes, and tend to concentrate on four main areas:

- internal communication – like keeping staff informed of important changes in the company. This may take the form of one-off specials or regular magazine-style programmes.

- external communication – keeping customers and the public informed and aware of the products and services offered by the company or organisation. This may well include public relations, for example.

- training – a key area here might be Health and Safety training programmes for the workforce or the introduction of new processes or working practices.

- sales and marketing – launching new products or services *to the trade,* for example.

Freelance employment opportunities – corporate production represents an important source of potential employment, almost half the workforce (48 per cent) is freelance. In addition, such companies can often provide good practical training for the inexperienced freelance who may well be required to fulfil a variety of roles in the production process. One slight note of caution, however, for those who intend to develop their freelance careers in the broadcast sector: corporate production may well be a good entry point into the industry for the newly qualified, but it is not always easy to move on. There is a tendency for those involved in corporate production and those in broadcast production to move in different circles both at work and at industry events outside work. Even outside London, the networks are rather different, and tend not to overlap. There is even a slight tendency in some broadcast circles to regard corporate production with a degree of superiority. There is no justification for this kind of professional snobbery and those whose businesses are primarily focused on the needs of industry deserve the respect due to those engaged in a demanding sector. On a more positive note, Skillset points out that corporate production is one of the fastest growing sectors in the UK economy – *turning over £2.7 billion in 2002. It is bigger than the entire UK film industry*.[26] Jobs available in this sector will run through the entire range from runner to executive producer and production managers as well as technical and craft grades like camera operator and editor. The ability to perform a variety of tasks might well be an advantage in this sector or the industry; those who can operate a camera as well as research and direct will probably find themselves much in demand.

The IVCA (International Visual Communication Association) is an industry association whose membership is open to clients, production companies and freelances. Like many other professional organisations it organises meetings and courses as well as providing networking opportunities.

FACILITIES AND HIRE

Facilities and Hire Companies perform a vital role throughout the industry by providing specialist equipment on a hire basis. Such equipment is usually of high value and costly to buy and maintain. Broadcasters, film and television production companies prefer to hire such equipment as required and not to purchase it outright. It will range from the camera and lenses to the less obvious specialist camera mounts, dollies and tracks, smoke machines and lighting. Companies usually specialise in the equipment and services they provide and include:

- cameras, lenses and mounts;
- outside broadcast equipment and vehicles;
- grip equipment such as tracks, dollies, jib arms;
- lighting;
- sound;

- physical special effects;

- pyrotechnic special effects;

- specialist transport and catering.

Freelance employment opportunities – about one-fifth of the workforce in this sector are freelance, and often come from specialised or technical backgrounds in electronic, broadcast video or audio engineering. Jobs include planning and coordination, on-site set up, installation rigging and maintenance as well as servicing and maintenance at base. Companies in this sector are also likely to be asked to supply the services of camera operators, vision-mixers (on outside broadcasts) audio engineers and, on occasions, producers and directors according to the client's needs.

POST-PRODUCTION

A vast array of post-production facilities exists to service the needs of programme makers. These can be categorised as

- editing facilities, providing both on-line and off-line facilities on, for example Avid non-linear (digital) suites. Such facility houses will usually provide equipment which is 'industry standard', in other words similar to that used by broadcasters and other production and post-production facilities. This gives the client confidence in the compatibility of standards at different points in the production process. The independent producer needs to demonstrate to the commissioner to whom he submits the final programme that the technical standards in post-production match the broadcaster's technical specifications.

- post-production audio, carrying out the final sound mix of the programme. This service may be provided by an editing facility (see above) or by a specialist audio production and post-production facility.

- graphics facilities for titling, illustration and credits may be provided by the edit house for simple and straightforward sequences. More commonly, however, title sequences will be designed and produced by specialist facilities using high-powered computers and special graphics programs operated by graphic designers with specialist skills and extensive experience of the production process.

Companies in the sector tend to be small or medium-sized enterprises with clients in commercial production, broadcast and corporate markets. Freelance work is certainly available throughout the post-production facilities sector, and will tend to be suitable for those with specialist experience or qualifications within a fairly narrow range of specialisms.

Freelance employment opportunities – about 15 per cent of the workforce in this sector are freelance. Opportunities arise at a variety of skill and experience levels. Many post-production houses will employ runners or trainees, or bring in extra help in junior positions if the work on hand requires it. At a more senior level, freelances may be employed as editors or senior editors and there may also be openings for sound, graphics and computer technicians.

INTERACTIVE MEDIA

This is not an easy sector to describe. In many ways it lies between corporate production and digital media production, and embraces elements of both. It would certainly describe the activities of a company which produced CD-ROMs or DVDs for:

- education;

- sales and marketing;

- internal and external communication;

- training;

- academic use;

- leisure and entertainment.

In some areas, website production which utilises many similar skills would also be seen as part of the interactive media sector. Because it is such a specialised area, it is not intended to cover online, web development and Internet services within the scope of this book. The difficulty in pinning down an exact definition of interactive media is an indication of one of the strengths of this sector. It is the result of what is best described as *convergence*, a coming together and blurring of distinction between media like radio and television and other digital technology such as the CD-ROM and DVD. The *interactive* part of the definition of interactive media refers to the fact that it is the user that controls the rate of the flow of information and the order in which that information is communicated. The use of interactive media is important because it can allow the producer to concentrate on the material to be communicated, and to choose the most effective way for it to be disseminated. A company wishing to inform its workforce about health and safety issues, for example, might commission a corporate video production to carry the message. Groups of employees might watch a ten-minute video and then discuss the issues which have been raised. On the other hand, a CD-ROM or DVD might use similar footage, digitised into much shorter sequences with accompanying text and graphics and targeted at individual workers to view and interact with at a time suitable to them. It does not take a great deal of imagination to conceive of the varying merits of these alternative applications and their different ways of communicating; the point is that the commissioner is free to decide on the most effective solution in any particular situation.

Freelance employment opportunities – It is not easy to identify the range of work that is available in this sector. Skillset figures reveal that more than 50,000 workers are employed, which makes interactive media the largest employment sector in the audio-visual industries. Of these workers, just under 20 per cent are freelance. The nature of the work undertaken is very varied and difficult to categorise and ranges from programming or interactive design engineering, to graphic design, camera operation and sound recording. In other words, all the skills, expertise and creativity that are found in the traditional media are required in the interactive media sector alongside some specific additional technical skills. The proliferation of small businesses engaged in this activity suggests that many of the individuals working in it are multi-skilled and probably enjoy a range of activity which is not confined to a single expertise. It is true to say that such multi-skilling is becoming increasingly prevalent in the audio-visual industries generally, but is probably particularly in evidence in this sector. In some ways, then, the appeal of work in this area will be polarised between specialists and generalists. The specialist may be required for very technical skills in the programming and design of the CD-ROM, for instance, and the generalists for the creation of the content.

7
Pitching ideas

DEFINITIONS

Commissioner – the representative of a broadcaster who is responsible for buying (and usually overseeing the production of) programme ideas in a particular genre of output.

Pitch – the act of setting out, elaborating and advancing a *proposal* (usually in person).

Proposal – a written (and usually brief) document outlining the nature, scope, content and cost of a suggested programme.

Treatment – that part of a *proposal* which sets out how the completed programme is intended to look or sound to its audience.

Synopsis – a concise account of the storyline of a programme.

Strand – a series of programmes which may include contributions from a variety of producers. An example of this would be the Channel 4 documentary series *Cutting Edge*. Such a *strand* provides an identifiable branding within a network's output.

INTRODUCTION

Many freelances have chosen to be freelances in the media industry because they want to be free to nurture their own creative programme ideas. This can be a difficult and fraught activity and it is certainly time consuming. It is one thing to have what you consider to be a really good, original and exciting idea in your head and quite another to put it down satisfactorily and briefly on paper. From the outset it is important to have a realistic approach to the whole process.

The vast majority of programme proposals to broadcasters never make it on to the air. The chance of a single one of your ideas being funded is very remote. Here lies the heart of the difficulty and frustration in making programme proposals. To do it successfully you have to be totally committed to your idea and its viability. On the other hand you need to be realistic and ready for disappointment. Keeping this balance is important not simply for your emotional and mental well-being but for your economic viability too. As we have already seen, persistence and tenacity are key qualities in the successful freelance, but knowing when to stop beating on a door which is firmly shut is an equally useful attribute. Moving on to propose new ideas might well be a better use of your time and energy than continuing to champion an idea that nobody wants or is prepared to commission.

It's worth remembering that a lack of interest in a particular proposal is only a rejection at this particular moment. Nothing is lost if you file your idea, only to dust it off in a year or two's time. Commissioners are notoriously fickle and very aware of the latest trends in popular programmes. It may well be that, at a different time and in a changed broadcasting environment, someone will leap at your proposal. The art is in knowing when to turn your energies elsewhere. The management of time for a freelance is an important matter and nowhere is this more apparent than when it comes to programme proposals.

Giving advice on preparing proposals is fraught with difficulty. Each guideline that can be elaborated will be contradicted by someone in the industry who can cite evidence or experience to show that following the opposite course of action can bring success. Should you slave over several drafts of your proposal document when someone tells you that a major series was commissioned for BBC2 from an idea sketched on the back of an envelope? Common sense must prevail. A producer who is fortunate enough to have a close relationship with a commissioner who trusts them is likely to be able to take shortcuts in the process which are simply not available to those who do not have an existing track record in the business.

It is helpful to think of the proposal in the same way as a CV or résumé; neither can guarantee success but, poorly presented, they may well precipitate failure. The proposal is your best chance of showing your ideas and creativity to their best advantage.

The guidance which follows can be modified as your experience of the commissioning process grows. You also need to take into account that different commissioners have their own ways of doing business. Some commissioning rounds are closed to all but a selected group of independent producers. Others will be open to all-comers.

THE COMMISSIONING PROCESS

Commissioning *rounds* – as they are generally described – are a regular feature of the broadcasting industry year, both in radio and television. Quite simply a *round* is the period which begins with a commissioner unveiling a shopping list of programmes or series they would like to commission. A closing date is usually

announced after which the commissioning editor discusses short-listed programmes in greater detail with the producers who have submitted the proposals.
The ability to submit is entirely at the discretion of the broadcaster and is usually
by invitation only. Commissioning practice varies between broadcasters. For some
commissions, only a selected number of companies will be invited to tender their
proposals. These will usually be those who have a track record in a particular
genre, or those with whom the commissioner has worked successfully before. On
other occasions there may be an open call for proposals. The term *open* should not
however be misunderstood. It is virtually impossible for a single individual
without a track record or background in the industry to successfully submit a proposal direct to a broadcaster or a commissioner. Although this may seem unfair,
even making modest programmes is an expensive and at times risky business.
Broadcasters require at least some confidence that the recipient of their funding
has the experience and skill to deliver a programme which is of high quality and
to deliver it on time. Almost invariably, then, programme proposals come to commissioners from established companies, or from established and trusted individuals working within companies.

To the outsider this can seem a daunting process and one which is impossible to
penetrate. Difficult, yes – impossible, no! To turn an idea (even a brilliant one) into
a programme ready for transmission requires a wide range of creative and
administrative skills which will usually only be found within a production unit in
an independent production company or a programme-making department of a
broadcaster. These production units have gathered skills and experience in a
particular programme genre or range of genres. An attentive radio listener or
observant television viewer will easily identify independent production companies
whose names regularly appear on the credits for specific genres. For an industry
outsider, or someone at the beginning of a freelance career, wise counsel would
suggest making first contact with an independent production company in the area.
It shouldn't be too difficult to speak briefly on the telephone to arrange a meeting
or to submit an idea in writing. On the whole, no producer or commissioner likes
to deal with growing piles of unsolicited programme ideas. Simply sending in your
idea probably isn't the best way to proceed.

Recently published research into the television commissioning process revealed that:

> There was widespread acknowledgement that very few unsolicited ideas
> were carried forward into commission, and that excessive time was spent
> on administering the processes required to deal with such submissions. The
> status quo is unsatisfactory to both parties; it creates an administrative
> headache for broadcasters and results in false hopes and wasted resources
> for producers.[27]

At the same time, it is worth noting that broadcasters are for the main part reluctant to refuse unsolicited proposals fearing no doubt that in doing so they could miss the next big idea! As in many areas of life, the right to be heard (or read) usually has to be earned. A good relationship with a production company is a helpful source of information when it comes to framing a programme proposal. Whatever the route you choose to promote your original programme idea, forming good relationships with industry professionals is an indispensable part of a successful strategy.

Painting a negative picture of the chances of breaking into the commissioning process is justified by the facts. The majority of ideas don't make it to through the commissioning process; hardly any unsolicited proposals reach the production stage. Despite this, there are success stories. Many people in the media industries have had to be determined and tenacious to succeed. Happily, many of them remember their early struggles and will often lend a helping hand to someone who is at the start of their career. This may take the form of advice or an introduction. If you are fortunate, a company might well decide to back your idea and help you to develop it and take it through the commissioning process. You will however still need a written proposal – and it should be as good as you can possibly make it!

SOURCES OF FUNDING

Broadcasters as commissioners will be the primary source of funding for most programme ideas. There are, however, other organisations in the UK who control significant programme-making funds. These will usually be based in the 'Nations and Regions', which is the way the industry describes Scotland, Wales and Northern Ireland, and the major production centres in England like Manchester, Birmingham and Bristol. Such organisations may well be the gateway to lottery and EU funding for film and television. Sometimes such funding will be for the entire programme budget; more often a partnership will be established with broadcasters on a percentage funding basis. A third way in which such agencies provide funding is in the form of development grants to enable individuals and production companies to engage in the research (and possibly scripting) they have to undertake to develop a programme idea. Lastly, special schemes or programmes are often in place on an occasional or annual basis to encourage new and emerging production and technical talent to make the first steps on the professional ladder. Schemes such as these are vitally important to those starting in the industry, not simply for the obvious financial benefits, but because of the back-up, support and advice they can provide. Because the number and type of such funds and schemes are extremely varied, the wisest course of action is to contact the relevant agency to discover what schemes might be appropriate for your needs. A list of such bodies is provided in Chapter 10.

WRITING THE PROPOSAL

There can be no hard and fast rules for writing this kind of document. Sometimes a commissioner may ask for your proposals in a particular form. If so, do as you are asked, no more, no less. More probably you'll simply be given a guide as to how much to write. If you're asked to provide one or two sides of A4 it would be foolish to write more thereby prompting the reader to ask why you can't follow simple instructions! There are some simple guidelines which ought to help you to write a clear and effective document.

Write in the present tense. This reinforces the idea of your programme as a concrete reality. 'This documentary tells the story of . . .' is more compelling and dynamic than 'This documentary would tell the story . . .', which sounds weaker and more tentative.

Keep sentences short. Again this will give your writing a more dynamic feel. Try to keep one thought per sentence and don't let your style ramble.

Use visual language. Remember that you want the reader to see pictures as they read your document. This is just as true for radio proposals as for television. You are attempting to convince a commissioner of your creative abilities. This should apply as much to your writing skills as to your directing or camera work.

Maintain a clear structure. Headings are particularly helpful in finding your way through a document. Similarly they help you to write the document in a clear, logical and sensible way. Headings help you to remember the major points your proposal should contain. If you prefer you can suppress all or some of the headings at a later stage when you are satisfied with what you have written.

Don't oversell. You must be confident that you can deliver what you promise if you wish to build any kind of reputation.

Don't use meaningless phrases. These include things like 'this will be a lively and entertaining programme' – of course it will, but the reader wants to know *how* you're going to make it lively and *who* it will entertain. I've lost count of the number of times I have read proposals which promised a *stylish* treatment of the subject and I still don't know what it means.

Be consistent throughout your document. It may seem obvious but you should not contradict yourself. For instance if you propose a target audience of young teenagers ensure that the material proposed in other parts of your document is consistently suitable for that audience.

The elements of the proposal

Essentially your proposal document should contain the following elements:

- the producer/company;

- programme title;

- target audience;

- synopsis or outline;

- treatment;

- notes.

In some circumstances you may also need to include:

- budget outline;

- schedule.

1 The producer/company

You may need to take at least a line or two to say who you are and to give brief details of your experience or track record. This is not the place to go into great detail. It may be important to let the reader know of the previous success and experience of the principal members of the team working on the programme. On the other hand, if you are well known to the commissioner then such information can be restricted to the basics.

2 Programme title

Producers spend many hours agonising over an appropriate and memorable title for a new programme or series. I know from personal experience just how difficult it can be to keep working on a pitch until you've found a title that seems satisfactory. One way around this is to adopt what is known as a *working title* as a temporary measure until you think of something better. Sometimes this will help to free up your mind to work constructively on the programme outline. Many people will tell you that the title doesn't matter – but it never feels that way when it's your programme proposal!

3 Target audience

You may include this information as part of the synopsis or set it out in a separate paragraph. You should specify carefully here which broadcaster your programme is pitched for. Remember that a programme is not likely to have universal appeal, but should commend itself to a particular audience. The audience sector can be identified in the usual demographic categories of age, gender, social class, etc. It may also be helpful to cite a specific time slot for the network as a way of defining your target audience. Take care to use the same audience categories the broadcaster uses both in terms of slot and target audience. There may well be good reasons that a broadcaster targets a specific slot for 7–13 year olds. You would ignore such established practices at your peril. A commissioner is not likely to take you seriously if you suggest a ten-minute documentary at 9 pm when he or she traditionally transmits a highly rated US drama series. If your proposal is in response to a specific request from a commissioner who has invited ideas for a particular programme slot or strand, then you would not need to repeat the information you have already been given, apart perhaps from a passing reference to indicate that you are aware of the demographics and target audience.

4 Synopsis or outline

Synopsis is a term most often used in fiction proposals where it refers to a précis of the main elements of the plot line or story. In other forms of programming, such as factual or documentary for example, either term can be and is used.

The outline is arguably the most important part of your document. This first paragraph might determine whether the commissioner reads on or consigns your idea to the reject pile. Above all you are preparing a *selling document*, and this may well be the only chance you will have to grab the attention of the commissioning editor or backer. Every word and every sentence must count. This is your opportunity to demonstrate your own grasp of the subject, your enthusiasm and commitment (but don't go over the top!).

The account of your concept should be about one-half to two-thirds of an A4 page, tightly and attractively written. Remember to specify, if you haven't done so already, whether this is a one-off programme or a series that you are proposing.

5 The treatment

The important thing that distinguishes the treatment from the concept is the point of view – now we only want to see the programme from the point of view of the audience, what they will see when the programme is transmitted. So you're painting pictures with words – language will be descriptive and visual.

This is the part of the proposal that gives, in broad brush strokes, the scope and range of the programme. Your starting point should be clear, as should your destination, so perhaps we are best to think of a sketch map of the journey you intend to undertake. Your strategy, hypothesis or argument should be perfectly clear and lucidly argued.

Again, with a broad brush, give an account of the principal and significant locations and participants. At this point the skill is to be specific and concrete and yet to allow yourself some flexibility and room for manoeuvre.

Literally, this is your opportunity to show how your subject will be treated, so you should be prepared to elaborate on:

Structure, e.g. a day in the life or the diary of a journey. This should reiterate what you have briefly touched on already in your coverage of the narrative in your concept.

Form and style, e.g. use of camera, interviews, voice-over, etc. You should elaborate on your overall approach; whether, for instance, the narrative will be provided by voice-over interview with questions removed or by a narrator. At this point you might usefully bear in mind the genre or sub-genre of programme you are making. Ensure that you are observing the conventions of the genre or, at any rate, show that you are aware of them!

6 Notes

The Notes section is your opportunity to cover important points not directly dealt with in the synopsis or treatment. Important areas to be dealt with might be agreements with artists or presenters or other participants (known in the business as *talent*) or special access you might have to people and places not normally available to programme makers. This may well give your proposal a special edge and you will need to draw this information to the attention of the commissioner.

A SAMPLE PROPOSAL

The following proposal has never been submitted and the production company is fictitious. The story which inspires it is, however, quite genuine. It appeared in the *Guardian* on 18 December 2003.

THE PICTURE

A ten-minute documentary film for the BBC 2 series *10 × 10**

Outline

The picture

A dusty and grainy archive photograph reprinted in an exhibition catalogue . . . 'It features a youngish couple, the woman carrying a handbag and a very young child. She peers off to one side, while her husband fiddles with what looks like a camera in its carrying bag. He is having difficulties, made worse by cigarette smoke curling into his eyes. He'd do better to throw it away and concentrate on the task in hand, before his encumbered wife takes offence.'

The photographer

In 1950, one of Britain's first female photojournalists, Grace Robertson, walked from her office to Trafalgar Square. There she took a striking photograph of a young family, father, mother and babe in arms. The photograph was published in the Picture Post. More than half a century later that same photograph appeared again – not only in an exhibition but in the exhibition catalogue.

The family

By a strange coincidence, related in the programme, the photograph came to the attention of Veronica Lee, the baby in the picture. No one in the family had any idea that it had been taken. The story of the photograph and the family it captured for that brief moment is told by Veronica Lee, the baby in the photograph and by Grace Robertson, the photographer.

Treatment

Rostrum camera explores this striking black and white photograph from grainy close-ups of the faces to the full shot with its Trafalgar Square background. Archive film footage adds to the Picture Post atmosphere of London in the fifties. The family's side of the story is told to camera and in voice over by Veronica Lee. The photographer, Grace Robertson, recalls the circumstances and the moment in which she came to take the photograph.

An engaging yet simple story of a photograph, a family, a coincidence and a celebrated photographer is simply recounted in this ten-minute documentary.

Notes

The main participants, Veronica Lee and Grace Robertson, have indicated their agreement in principle to take part in the programme. Discussions have taken place with a view to obtaining permission to use the photograph which should present no problem.

* BBC2's *10 X 10* was an occasional series which offered an opportunity for directors with no previous network directing credit to make low budget ten-minute fiction or documentary films for broadcast on BBC2. It commissioned ten films per series. Successful applicants were provided with production finance and practical guidance by the BBC Bristol Features Department.

PROTECTING YOUR IDEAS – COPYRIGHT

This section is intended as a very brief introduction and guide to a very complex and specialist area. If you have real concerns about copyright and the theft of your intellectual property then the proper course of action is to consult a lawyer, and possibly one specialising in media or copyright issues. There are a few points, however, that can be made to give a general summary of the issues involved.

Copyright is a legal issue

Copyright law is enshrined in a number of statutes. You should bear in mind that when Parliament acts, the law changes, so ensure you have up-to-date information. The Copyright, Designs and Patents Act 1988 is the main UK law governing copyright matters. Additionally, the UK is subject to European legal directives. Amendments to UK law (described by the Patent Office as largely technical) were made late in 2003 to bring it fully into compliance with EU requirements.

Copyright is about property

In this case the property is what is known as *intellectual property*, the result of work energy and time that an individual has devoted to a particular work. The notion of *a work* is significant; copyright exists in such work and not in ideas. It follows, then, that the more development that goes into a programme idea, the more possible it will become to establish copyright. It is not enough, therefore, to have an idea about a programme on railways in the nineteenth century – the idea would need to be developed in some distinctive way with a recognisably original format. If someone else has a similar railway idea and gets it accepted by a broadcaster, it is unlikely that you would be able to demonstrate that it has infringed your copyright. In other words, you would not be able to show that the other party had *copied* your original work.

Establishing copyright

There is no official registration of copyright in the UK. There are, however, a number of ways in which you can assert copyright on your own work.

You could post a copy of the proposal or outline to yourself using recorded delivery or a similar system. On delivery you would retain the envelope *unopened* until required. Other variations on this theme could involve depositing the envelope with a solicitor or in a bank vault. One useful tip is to sign and date the envelope across the seal and then cover the seal with adhesive tape.

A number of agencies will now accept outlines and scripts for timed and dated safekeeping for copyright purposes. These agencies do provide useful and free information on their websites, though they do make a charge for registering your scripts or outlines. Two such private agencies are The Script Vault and The UK Copyright Service.

The copyright symbol © can be used to mark your script. Though this is not strictly necessary in the UK, it does indicate that you take the protection of your intellectual property seriously.

It is also worth noting that all terrestrial broadcasters in the UK have agreed a code of practice with the Alliance for the Protection of Copyright.[28] The code specifically deals with the protection of material submitted to commissioners.

Although the terms *copyright* and *patent* should not be confused, the government-run Patent Office has a great deal of useful free information on copyright matters. Most of this is available online, www.patent.gov.uk/.

8
Business matters

In this world nothing can be said to be certain, except death and taxes.
Benjamin Franklin in a letter to Jean Baptiste Le Roy

The aim of this chapter is to try to map the business skills which are required by all freelances, and to chart the main issues with which you need to be familiar. This is not meant to be a business manual, but a guide to alert you to things you need to know about, whether or not you are setting up a company of any kind. As before, if any of the points raised here are of concern to you, then you should seek professional advice.

It will have become clear by now that embarking on a freelance career, and, more importantly, sustaining it, requires a good deal of careful planning and decision making. Inevitably the freelance who is accepted by the tax authority as self-employed is in effect running a business and is required by law to do so in an efficient way, by keeping proper records and submitting appropriate returns. Essentially the freelance is supplying personal skills and services, often including the supply of equipment used by the freelance in order to do the job. In such a case, the contractual relationship of the freelance is with the company (an independent production company, for example) who engages the freelance. That company, in its turn, will be engaged in a contract with the end user or commissioner. A sound recordist, for example, may be engaged as a freelance to work for an independent production company which, in turn, is itself working on a programme the company is making for Channel 4.

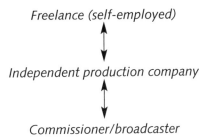

Freelance (self-employed)

↕

Independent production company

↕

Commissioner/broadcaster

As we shall see, this apparently simple arrangement masks a multitude of relationships and networks which the self-employed freelance must maintain to the satisfaction of all parties. This chapter will deal with the important business issues which, like it or not, the freelance has to deal with in the course of work. So this concerns you, the freelance, not as a skilled and creative media professional, but as a business-person. The chapter goes on to deal with the issues involved when the business of being a freelance grows and moves from being a one-person business (known legally as a sole trader) to one which involves other people in a more or less formal business relationship. This relationship might be in the form of a partnership (can be quite informal) or a limited company (formal). It is, of course, a matter of contention whether a director of a limited company could properly be regarded as a freelance, but as we have seen, there is no sharp, legal or agreed definition as to what a freelance actually is. If being a freelance is one way of initiating and growing a career in the audio-visual industries, then turning that career into a business may be a way of further establishing and securing it.

This chapter should be read in the context of Chapter 1, which deals with the issues of defining a freelance and the nature of the tax status of individuals working in radio and television in that capacity.

WHAT KIND OF BUSINESS?

Usually, a business start-up will be a relatively small affair, but it is still very important to work out what *legal form* your business is going to take, and there are four basic choices:

- sole trader;

- partnership;

- limited company;

- limited liability partnership.

Sole trader: according to the Skillset census of 2003, around 7 per cent of freelances (defined as those working on contracts of less than 365 days a year) were operating as sole traders. This is the simplest way of carrying on a business. There is no special legal framework and the business and the individual running it are virtually indistinguishable. Paperwork is simple and there are no complex legal returns to be made to the Registrar of Companies. If the business runs into problems, those problems are your problems and you are legally liable for them, debts as well as profits!

Partnership: essentially similar to a sole trader but with two or more people involved. The most important thing to remember about a partnership is that all members of it are *jointly and severally liable*. This rather high-flown legal phrase means that if one of the partners fails to pay any debts incurred by the partnership, the remaining partners are liable for that partner's share. In other words, one person could become liable for the whole debt of the business. This may sound alarming, but although you need to take care, many of the problems can be overcome by having a proper partnership agreement drawn up by a lawyer. The partnership agreement should detail the role of each partner, the money put in to the business, how voting on decisions is carried out and so on, covering most eventualities, even how the partnership would be wound up and any profits shared.

Limited company: this is a separate legal entity, and quite distinct from those who work in it or who own it – the shareholders. It can be a private limited company (Ltd) or a public limited company (plc), although very few start-ups begin life as a plc! One advantage of this form is that the company itself is liable for business debts, and shareholders are only risking the value of the shares they own. Whilst this seems an ideal solution, and a shelter from personal responsibility if the business folds up, in reality the situation is not quite this easy. Any institution lending money would almost certainly require personal guarantees from the directors as well as taking security over the assets of the company. There are some advantages in setting up a limited company. It tends to be taken seriously by clients because your financial accounts have to be submitted to Companies House and are available for inspection. A limited company makes it rather easier for someone who is not working for the company to invest in it.

Limited liability partnership: this has elements of both a limited company and a partnership. It is a new form of business which only came into existence in 2001. It was introduced as a way of benefiting from the advantages of limited liability whilst allowing the conduct of the business to be carried on in much the same way as a traditional partnership. Such partnerships do have to be registered at Companies House.

There are certain other forms of business it might be worth considering, these would include co-operatives or employee-owned businesses, as well as community owned businesses. As with all business start-ups, the best advice is to get advice from the specialists. More information is provided later in this chapter and in the reference section of this book.

BUSINESS ISSUES FOR ALL FREELANCES

Insurance

This is probably the first thing you should think about before you engage in any freelance work. Interestingly, the first priority is not primarily to safeguard your own interests, but to safeguard those of others. In doing so, however, you will be looking after yourself albeit indirectly.

Public liability insurance is designed to protect you in the event that you cause injury to a third party (somebody else). A camera operator, for example, might leave a tripod unattended on the ground during a shoot. A member of the public walks by and, not noticing the tripod, trips over it and sustains an injury. If the injured party sues, the freelance needs to be insured to meet a claim if a court holds the camera operator liable for damages. Similar situations might also arise where injury or damage to property is involved; again public liability insurance is required to protect the freelance. Operating without such insurance is a very risky and ultimately foolhardy decision. It does not take a great deal of imagination to foresee the many circumstances in which serious incidents can arise. If damages are awarded against you and you have neither insurance nor the money to pay, you are in danger not only of losing the business but any other assets that you might have – and that could include your home. This is very basic insurance and should be regarded as absolutely essential. Many trade unions and professional associations offer such insurance at discounted rates as a benefit of membership. This is worth considering, as the policies negotiated are usually structured to take into account the particular needs of those involved in a particular sector of the audio-visual industries.

Employee liability insurance is essential – and, more importantly, is a legal requirement for anyone who employs anyone else. That employee may be injured in the course of their employment and the employer might well be liable. This situation could arise if a sound recordist, for example, engages the services of an assistant whilst carrying out work for someone else. If you pay someone in these circumstances, then the law would usually consider that there is a contract of employment – written or otherwise. If things go wrong and you are deemed to be the employer, you would be liable and you would need the insurance. As the law stands at present, the minimum cover required is for £5 million. This is not an expensive insurance to buy, and again trade unions and professional associations might have specially negotiated rates to offer their members.

Personal insurance. Under this category you should think very carefully about your own personal situation as a freelance. What would happen if you have an accident, are injured or fall ill? You will not be able to work. For a short period finances might survive, a prolonged period may prove catastrophic. It is virtually certain that state benefit of any kind would not cover the losses you would incur. A range of policies is available to cover these eventualities. Premiums for policies to cover these situations are not cheap but the risk of not insuring against them is probably not worth taking. Polices to cover these kinds of personal and family risks are sold under a variety of names and each approaches the cover in a slightly different way. To ascertain which policy or combination of policies is right for your particular circumstances, you should investigate:

- income protection insurance;

- critical illness insurance;

- key man insurance;

- private health insurance.

Other kinds of insurance are perhaps a little more obvious and straightforward, but nonetheless crucial.

- Motor vehicles. It is vital that the insurer knows that you intend to use the vehicle in the course of your business. This is different from cover given for journeys to and from a place of employment. If you intend to carry equipment or tools of the trade or if you carry other people like presenters or actors, your premium will be affected. If you fail to tell your insurer about these things, you may well find that, in the event of a claim, you will not be covered.

- Premises. You may not have an office, but if you carry out work from home, it would be wise (and probably part of the *small print* in your policy), to inform your insurer, especially if you keep items of equipment there.

- Equipment. Anything you use as part of your work is unlikely to be insured as part of any household policy. You should itemise it and insure it separately.

Life as a freelance is characterised by uncertainty and vulnerability; insurance is an important way of assessing risk and safeguarding against this vulnerability. Advice on insurance can usually be obtained free, but you should take care that it comes from an impartial source. An Internet search can provide information on most kinds of insurance, and trade unions and professional groups generally have a great deal of information and advice on offer. If you have a wide range of insurance needs, a broker might be helpful and, in some circumstances, can save money on premiums. Professional advice is worth having on such a crucial matter which involves your professional and personal well being and security and that of your co-workers and family.

Pensions (or retirement income)

There has been a great deal of talk in the press and on radio and television about a 'pensions crisis'. The failure of a number of company pension schemes has left a small but significant number of employees close to retirement with nothing to supplement the state pension. Coupled with the anxiety that the value of the state pension has been seriously eroded, such problems have led to much debate and a great deal of anxiety. All this has been compounded by the well-publicised problems of certain financial institutions and allegations of mis-selling. No wonder then that pension planning is hardly at the top of the agenda for those starting a freelance career. Indeed it seems as if it is not much of a priority even for those who are well advanced on their career paths. The Trades Union Congress (TUC) pointed out in mid-2004 that less than half of those under thirty were saving for a pension.[29] Some financial advisers would go so far as to suggest that pension plans as such are possibly not the best way to ensure a reasonable income in retirement. Clearly this is a matter of opinion and it is certainly not within the scope of this book to attempt financial advice. What is beyond contention, however, is the advisability of taking seriously the question of planning for retirement income, whatever means are used to generate that income. Freelance workers have no company or kindly employers to make contributions on their behalf, so it's up to you to take responsibility for your own future and all financial advisers would agree that the earlier you start, the better will be the results. Pension provision is a rather complicated area, the language can be confusing and some state provisions have changed both in name and in nature!

What follows is intended as a basic map of the world of pensions, with the strong advice that you should take the whole issue seriously and get a more detailed map and a reliable guide in the shape of a financial adviser.

- *The Basic State Pension* is provided as a result of the contributions made through National Insurance Contributions. Entitlement is not automatic and depends on the level of contributions that have been made. In 2004 it amounts to less than £80 a week.

- *The Pension Credit* recognises that the Basic State Pension is not enough to live on and, therefore, in the absence of savings of more than £6,000 will top up the weekly pension to just over £100 for a single person.

- *The Additional State Pension* used to be called SERPS (or State Earnings Related Pension). It is sometimes referred to by the title S2P. It is, as the name suggests, a second state pension designed to give better benefits to those on low or modest incomes. It is possible to opt-out of paying contributions to this scheme if you join a company pension scheme, a stakeholder or a personal pension scheme. The decision to opt-out is an important one which should not be taken without professional advice.

- *Company pension schemes* or occupational pensions are those set up by employers. In the past the employer did not have to offer such a scheme, but if it *were* offered then the employer was legally obliged to contribute to it. Changes in the law now mean that any company with more than five employees has to offer a scheme, but is not obliged to contribute to it. It may seem rather strange to embark on a description of occupational pension schemes to which, by definition, a freelance is unlikely to have access. However, many freelances may well have a history of full-time permanent employment earlier in their career. If this is the case, there may well be pension rights in a company scheme and therefore a decision has to be made on whether or not to transfer those rights into another, personal pension plan for example. Again this is a decision which calls for professional financial advice and one which should not be taken without a great deal of detailed thought and discussion.

- *Stakeholder pensions* are part of a government initiative to make pensions simpler and more attractive to a wider range of workers. An employer with more than five workers is obliged to offer a stakeholder pension scheme. The employer does not have to make a contribution to it and the workers do not have to join the scheme; indeed, if they don't like the scheme they are offered, they are free to choose another one. The distinctive feature of the stakeholder pension is that rules on how it works are set by the government and this includes the management fees that can be levied by the financial institutions selling the product. The maximum fee is currently 1.5 per cent. The stakeholder pension must be portable, so it goes with you when you move jobs and you can move from scheme to scheme without penalty. It is also possible to stop and start payments as circumstances demand which again might be an attractive feature for the freelance worker. The wisdom of seeking professional financial advice cannot be too highly stressed.

- *Personal pensions* are any pensions taken out by you as an individual. A large variety of financial institutions offer personal pensions, sometimes also referred to as private pensions. The key features of personal pensions for the freelance are portability and a degree of flexibility about contributions, depending on the rules of the particular scheme. How well a pension performs depends on the skill of the investment managers running the scheme and the buoyancy of the economy at any given time.

Keeping the books

Even for the most basic level of self-assessment tax returns, the law requires you to keep records. The Inland Revenue says you should keep all papers relating to self-assessment for a minimum of five years, and for VAT the period extends to six years. So there is no choice; if you are engaged in business you have to keep financial records. There are, however, many other good reasons apart from legal constraints for good book-keeping and record-keeping. Granted, this involves some dry routine on a daily, weekly or monthly basis, but the information such records can yield are of far more value to you than they are to the tax or VAT authorities. Book-keeping gives you an accurate snapshot of your finances and an ability not only to assess how your business has been performing, but how it is likely to perform in the future. At the most basic level it provides information about who you owe money to, and, even more importantly, who owes you money! Such records allow you to analyse where your money is being spent, and may prompt some decisions about economies or impel a negotiation with a supplier about a bigger level of discount to such a loyal customer. Record-keeping is not simply about past transactions, it forms the basis of planning and budgeting. Any bank or financial institution considering a loan will want to ensure that a prospective borrower is keeping accurate records, and will use those records in coming to its decision. Fortunately reasonably priced software is available which, even if it doesn't make book-keeping fun, can at least take some of the drudgery out of it. The two market leaders for basic book keeping which are suitable for the individual as well as the small business are Quicken from Intuit[30] and Microsoft Money.[31] Both programmes cover a similar range of functions and the choice is really a matter of personal taste and the particular requirements of the individual concerned. Both have associated programmes which help in the preparation of self-assessment forms for the Inland Revenue. There is, of course, a range of software available from a variety of manufacturers and suppliers and professional advice should be sought, especially if you have an accountant who might well have a view on the kind of software he would recommend.

Choosing an accountant

It is probably best to assume that you need an accountant, even though you may just be starting as a freelance or are involved in a start-up business. Obtaining the services of an accountant need not be an expensive matter, and for a new business or a fairly small enterprise you should be able to anticipate fees of less than £500 a year. There are ways too of keeping down these bills. Good record-keeping on your part saves an accountant time and reduces your bill if he or she doesn't have to hunt through boxes of un-filed receipts and bills to find some important piece of information. It is perhaps wise to choose an accountant who is based not too far away, saving expensive travelling costs for both parties. One tip well worth following is to ask around friends and colleagues in the business to see if they can recommend an accountant. They may be able to give you a notion of the fees you can expect. More importantly they may be able to tell you of an accountant with experience of and an understanding of the peculiarities of the audio-visual industries. It is also worth checking with local union branches or professional associations for similar information. Remember that it will be better to approach an accountant well before your first tax return is due. As deadlines approach, accountants become busier and burdened by last minute rushes and demands from their clients. A new freelance or start-up business needs and deserves a little more time!

Tax

Income tax. Every worker has a relationship with the tax authority, the Inland Revenue. For the freelance this will usually be through the self-assessment procedure. Schedule D is the tax schedule under which a self-employed person's profits are assessed. Starting out as a freelance you (or your accountant) need to tell the local Inland Revenue and seek self-employed status. There is, in fact, a list issued by the Revenue which details all the jobs in the audio-visual industries that they regard as legitimately self-employed. If your job or grade is not on this list, then anyone employing you has instructions to deduct tax and national insurance 'at source', in other words, before you get the money. It is of course possible to challenge the Inland Revenue rules and to put forward a case for you to be regarded as self-employed. To do this, you really need the help of an accountant or trade union representative with experience in this area. Self-employed status enables you to claim any expenses you incur wholly and exclusively in carrying out your work and set them against any tax you may owe.

The self-assessment system requires you to send in a return by specified dates and failure to do so incurs an automatic fine. Let us suppose, for example, that the tax year in question runs from 6 April 2003 and ends on 5 April 2004. If you wish the tax authority to work out how much you owe, your return must be submitted by the last day of September 2004. If you, your accountant or the computer software you have purchased is doing the computation, then you have until 31 January 2005. The annual cycle always refers to the tax year for the period ending on 5 April. In addition, of course, you have to make payments. The only problem about leaving your self-assessment return to the last possible moment (31 January) is that this is the date by which you also have to pay what you owe. And the matter does not end there, because in the following July you will probably be required to make an interim payment or payment on account. This is usually 50 per cent of what it is estimated that you will owe for the current year. If the estimate is wrong, then the amount will be balanced out when you make your next payment. It is worth remembering that, if the tax you owe turns out to be less than a specified amount (currently £2,000), the Revenue will arrange to collect this through the PAYE (Pay As You Earn) system. Clearly this is only going to be of help if you are on PAYE. This would be the case if, for example, you had a part-time permanent job and supplemented your earnings with free-lance work. In order to benefit from having tax you owe collected in this way, your self-assessment form needs to be completed and returned by the earlier date, the end of September.

Corporation tax. Although this may sound a little scary and out of the league of most people, it is simply the tax paid by companies. So, if your freelance work has turned into a small business, then you may well be liable to pay corporation tax.

National Insurance contributions are, to all intents and purpose, a tax too. In other words, you have no choice, you have to pay them and you cannot opt out! This is the contribution you make towards the cost of the health service, sick pay and all other aspects of social security provided by the state. Confusingly there are two sets of contributions payable by the freelance. The first are known as Class 2 contributions, and are at a flat rate. Although the cost is not great, about £2.50 per week, arrears can quickly mount up if contributions are not paid regularly. It is, however, possible to arrange to make regular payments by direct debit. The second group of payments is known as Class 4 contributions, these are based on the level of profit made by your business.

VAT. If your turnover as a freelance or small business is over a certain amount, (currently £50,000) then you are obliged to register for VAT (Value Added Tax). You will be issued with a VAT number and will be obliged to collect tax on behalf of HM Customs and Excise. At the current rate this will entail adding $17\frac{1}{2}$ per cent to your outgoing invoices. This money you collect has to be paid back to Customs but you are able to deduct the VAT you have paid on purchases for the business. There are various schemes for carrying out these transactions but, in most cases, a quarterly return is completed and at the end of each quarter this return is used to compute the amount owing to the VAT authority or, in some cases, to be reclaimed from them. The money is paid each quarter and there are penalties for late payment or for non-payment of sums due.

A final word on taxes. Probably the worst thing that any individual or business can do is to avoid the issue of taxes. Both the Inland Revenue and HM Customs and Excise take a serious view of any kind of evasion, non-payment or late payment. Both have very strong powers to enforce the law, and in some cases have more authority to search premises and seize goods and records than do the police. Any avoidance on your part only puts off an inevitable confrontation and will allow debts to increase by the addition of penalties and possibly fines. Ensure you register your activities with the authorities and complete whatever formalities are required. If you experience difficulty with making payments it is never advisable to hope that the problems will go away; they won't – they will get worse. Contacting the relevant authority will usually result in the situation being resolved and a payment plan can be initiated. It is, however, a good idea not to repeat the mistakes and to presume too much on goodwill and forbearance! Again, the soundest advice in this area is to consult your accountant or adviser at an early stage before matters get out of hand. If all this makes the tax authorities seem a little draconian, the final word is one of recommendation. The Inland Revenue maintains an excellent website and is a very good source of a wide range of advice for business start-ups. This advice extends to free publications which may be requested by post or downloaded online.[32]

Financial advice

Choosing a financial adviser is probably an even more crucial decision than finding the right accountant. It is important that you are aware that there are, at present, two types of financial adviser and that you are aware to which type any adviser you speak to belongs.

Tied advisers will only sell financial products from the company they are tied to and, although they have to give the best advice based on your own particular circumstances, they naturally will be looking at a narrower range of financial products.

Independent financial advisers (IFA) are not tied to a particular financial services company and are free to present a range of options, again geared to the particular needs of a client. IFAs are regulated by the Financial Services Authority (FSA) who maintain lists of authorised advisers and can give advice to help to find the right adviser.[33] Another government organisation, Business Link, has been set up by the Department of Trade and Industry (DTI) to give business support information and advice. In the section dealing with obtaining financial advice it suggests a number of useful questions to ask when choosing an independent financial adviser:

- Do they have expertise in your required area (pensions, investment, mortgages etc.)?

- Can you obtain recommendations and references?

- What is the extent of ongoing support after your needs have been insured?

- How is the IFA rewarded?[34]

This last point refers to the fact that IFAs have to earn a living and they may do so by charging a fee for their services or by obtaining a commission on financial products they sell to you. You need to ascertain on what basis your IFA proposes to operate. Although a commission basis appears to be free to the user, you should be aware that the costs will be reflected in charges you pay for your product together with set-up and ongoing operating costs. Finally, in choosing a financial adviser, Business Link suggests that you consider:

- personal recommendations;

- industry bodies or associations;

- insurance industry recommendations;

- the Internet.

The Financial Services Authority has proposed to introduce a third tier of financial adviser similar in kind to the tied adviser described above. This multi-tied adviser would be linked to a number of companies depending of the product specified, but as yet no agreement has been reached on the implementation of this proposal.

Some useful information including ways of finding lists of financial advisers is given in the reference section in Chapter 10 of this book.

SOURCES OF FUNDING AND BUSINESS ADVICE

Most businesses need money at the outset, known as start-up capital. For a small business growing out of freelance work, the requirement will probably be quite modest. A check list of the needs of the business may reveal a larger sum than sheer guesswork would indicate. Premises may be needed and a deposit for a lease has to be found. Transport and office equipment can cost a considerable sum, so it is worth drawing up a list and making a fairly accurate estimate of start-up costs. Having done that, the question inevitably arises as to where the money is to be found. If you have savings then it might be a good idea to invest at least some of them in the future of your business. You are likely to look after your finances more conscientiously if it is your own money that is being spent!

More than likely you will need to look for a modest external loan to help set up the business.

Banks and other financial institutions may well be willing to help with a small loan or business overdraft. Most banks have special departments focused on the needs of small businesses and business start-ups. Any high street branch will probably have literature available and may even have a small business adviser based in the branch. An Internet search will also reveal a wealth of banking advice, and 'start-up' packs abound. One of the most useful components of all these packs is a template for writing up a business plan. This is certainly worth doing, however modest your plans. It is unlikely that a bank would advance funds without seeing your plan.

Charities and Trusts can be a particularly helpful source, not only of funds but of advice and mentoring. Particularly worth mentioning are the Prince's Trust, and its Scottish counterpart, the Prince's Scottish Youth Business Trust. Fortunately the definition of youth is quite wide and generous, though in Scotland slightly less so! You can apply for assistance in England and Wales if you are aged from eighteen to thirty; in Scotland, the upper age limit is twenty-five. For those with a disability the applicable age range in Scotland is twenty-six to thirty. There's a comprehensive range of help available in the form of grants and loans, but probably the most useful features are help with:

- test marketing;

- pre-start training and advice;

- access to a business advisor for at least two years;

- book-keeping training and free book-keeping system;

- business competitions;

- PR;

- networking.

This is a very good scheme for college and university leavers who wish to set themselves up in business and find it difficult to raise funds or to pay for advice. Additionally the Prince's Trust aims to give continuing support to help businesses to grow and prosper and, to that end, development funding may also be made available.

Start-up schemes are often in place in a variety of shapes, sizes and names in universities and colleges specifically to help nurture new businesses set up by recent graduates. The existence and nature of such help will vary from institution to institution but it will certainly be worth your while to make local enquiries.

Development Agencies are probably the best starting point for your research into the help that is available to businesses in your area. These agencies exist in all areas of the UK.

- Regional Development Agencies in England[35]

  - West Midlands
  - East of England
  - East Midlands
  - London
  - One North East
  - North West
  - South East
  - South West
  - Yorkshire Forward

- Scottish Enterprise[36]

- Welsh Development Agency[37]

- Invest Northern Ireland.[38]

The best possible advice I could offer anyone contemplating setting up in business on their own account is to seek the best possible advice. The agencies listed above are a good starting point.

FREELANCE PERSPECTIVE

The following case studies concern two small companies set up specifically to provide employment for those setting them up. In both cases the companies started trading shortly after their founders graduated, both are located outside the South East of England.

Company A

This company was founded by two graduates in 2000 as a partnership. One of them had tried to get a runner's job, but at the going rate of £9K didn't feel that this was a viable start to a career in the media. The other partner was fortunate enough to win a scholarship to study the industry in America for a year and so the business marked time during his absence with the remaining partner doing free-lance work within another sector of the audio-visual industry to keep himself going financially.

Company aims – to pursue commissions in factual programming preferably in the documentary field and to work in the corporate sector whilst developing ideas and raising funding for the documentary project.

Start-up experience – they discovered that the local enterprise company could give them useful preliminary advice and a basic start-up course was very helpful because they met other people setting up businesses. Some of the people they came into contact with had been running businesses successfully for a little while. The partners were very enthusiastic about the practical help they had received from the Prince's Scottish Youth Business Trust. Because they received a £5,000 loan from the Trust, they had to agree to regular follow-up meetings with their business mentor throughout the life of the loan. They felt that this imposed a helpful discipline in the way they ran the business. They still keep in touch with the organisations which helped them set up the business. They used their start-up cash to buy a decent digital camera and a computer with a professional editing package. These were good buys, they explained:

> We can't afford the high cost of edit suite rental, and it's not viable for us even to go to a hire company for a camera.

They would have liked a little more capital at the beginning, but were reluctant to take on more loans:

> Taking on loans is a problem if you have student loans to be paid off – even if they've been deferred.

Company achievements – from the outset the work done has provided a living for each of the partners who have used some of their profits to modestly enhance their range of equipment.

The work we've done has been mostly corporate or educational although the idea [at the outset] was to branch out, to be creative.

The company has moved into bright, attractive accommodation, which is small but smart and in keeping with the image they are seeking to promote.

Reservations – although they still intend to pursue the creative documentaries idea, they find it difficult to make the time for it:

There's a big conflict between the corporate and the creative work that you'd like to develop . . . there's no great buzz about some corporates, but they do pay the wages!

Important lessons learned

Remember to place a value on the skills you've learned and that they're worth paying for.

Don't undersell yourselves. Some see video as a cheap novelty. You don't want to lose the job . . . it's difficult.

Company B

This limited company has been in existence for just over a year, since a group of five friends graduated and decided to work together.

We just couldn't help it . . . working together . . . too good to let it go.

Company aims – like Company A, the start up ambitions for this group were to make money and to try to combine creative and corporate work whilst developing their ideas. They would ultimately like to specialise in music videos and to develop scripts for short films and documentaries.

Start-up experience – the group were given some help at the outset to get them going. Essentially they were provided with a workspace and a telephone and were also awarded a £3,000 start-up grant. Now, a year later, the company has lost one of its founders after some disagreement about business style. To save money they are, for the time being, operating from the house one of them owns. None of them works full time in the business and they all have to do other work to make ends meet.

Over a year we've grown cynical, we realise it's not just round the corner to do what you want.

Financially, however, they are not too concerned:

We've grown closer together . . . earning some money . . . not a huge amount.

Company achievements – over the year they have developed an interest in video for the music business:

> we got backing to make a music video which has been seen all over Europe on MTV. It's very thrilling to see your own stuff on TV.

They have also been successful in developing an idea for video CVs for children with learning difficulties and have been nominated for an award:

> we've had great feedback from the teachers . . . it seems to have given the pupils a lot of confidence.

Reservations – the members of the company have had some difficult experiences, mainly with their treatment at the hands of potential clients:

> Cynical! We trusted everyone, but nothing is for free. Up 'til now we had been cocooned. Some people take your time. Potential clients took advantage, everyone knows you've just started.

Important lessons learned

> You need to take yourselves seriously otherwise people will take advantage of you.

> Don't expect to get rich!

> Think long-term and don't expect to have free time.

> Sometimes it's very helpful to cooperate [with other companies] but trust is a problem, you have to be careful.

Interestingly, this group were less impressed by the business help and advice they had received:

> We weren't business students; we had no business training, though two of us went on a marketing course.

> You're not in any position to check out those who are giving you business advice. Contact [with business adviser] was very vague, then one of the liaison people left.

Reflecting on experience

The experience of these two companies and of others I have spoken to highlights some concerns which would possibly not have occurred to me otherwise; though, on reflection, I had encountered them when running my own business. The benefit of other people's experience is that it helps to raise your own awareness of some of the pitfalls and problems that may confront you should you decide to set up a business as a way of developing your work.

Inexperience and underpricing – we have already seen in earlier chapters of this book that the freelance can be very vulnerable to many pressures; the same is true of young or start-up companies. I don't think that it is coincidental that these two companies both highlighted the problem of a tendency to undersell yourself; not to insist on the going rate for work you are doing. This is a hard one to get right because you are anxious to obtain the work, and the temptation is always to secure it by keeping your price low. The difficulty of this approach is that it's almost impossible to raise the price once you've started out low. Ultimately you have less to spend on the project and you make less profit. If this continues, there is a danger that the quality of your work will be compromised, or that you go out of business. There is no easy answer to the problem, but some practical principles may help.

- *Don't work for free.* It's not good business practice and will in any case give you a poor reputation in the business. Working speculatively on the basis that you'll get paid if the client's project is successful rarely brings in any money at all and there is no reason for you to take the risk. Sometimes such a venture may be justified, but as a rule it's never right for a new business. It takes too much time and distracts you from the business of making money from your projects.

- *Think carefully about your negotiating skills.* In a company engaged in audio-visual production, such skills may be as important as the skills you deploy to make your programme. It is possible that someone involved in the business has talents that lie in this direction. If so you should take advantage of them and if possible take steps to develop them. Don't be reluctant to go outside the company. If you know someone you respect for their negotiating skills and you can trust them, ask them to do the deals for you. You can arrange a flat rate fee or a small percentage cut to reward them. The advantage of this approach is that it allows the creative relationship with the client to continue unfettered by awkward discussions about money and terms.

- *Research your potential clients.* It doesn't pay to be naïve or too trusting in business. It is quite often relatively easy to make discreet enquiries about a client or potential client. If claims about contacts are made, ask yourselves if there's any way they can be confirmed. It is also worth remembering the old adage that if it's too good to be true, it probably isn't!

The quality of business advice – this book and especially this chapter have been at pains to underline the importance of professional advice. In as far as an outsider can judge, both the quality and the degree of advice experienced by the two companies profiled here has been rather different. Company A seems to have had more relevant support on a closer basis over a longer period of time. Paradoxically a system which provided a loan seemed also to provide a degree of oversight and discipline which an organisation providing a grant did not. This experience has suggested some further pointers.

- *Choose your advisers carefully.* Of course this is easier said than done. It looks as if the easier option is not always the best one for a business start-up. A number of organisations like the Prince's Trust have a great deal of experience in helping young people to set up business. This experience has enabled them to evolve a system of monitoring and mentoring which can often help to keep a business going in the right direction. Many organisations such as these will not authorise loans until basic tasks like business and marketing plans have been completed. It could well be that this modest degree of externally imposed business discipline is invaluable at the start-up stage.

- *Try some hard questions.* You are free to ask potential mentors or others about their own business experience. This is not necessarily a rude or insensitive question; you need to make sure there is a good match between your needs and the expertise of your adviser. It would do no harm to ask yourself this question: 'If he (or she) is so good, why is he not out making his next million?' In case this seems excessively suspicious I should point out that there can be completely reasonable answers to the question; I merely suggest that you need to feel confident that they are valid. You should also try to ascertain the level of support you can expect and how long it might continue, and if there is any kind of ongoing review available.

Creativity versus crust! – A problem facing many start-up businesses is how to find the time and energy to develop creative ideas whilst obeying the imperative to earn your daily bread. It is certainly unwise to deny that the problem exists. Clearly the experience of these two companies highlights the difficulty and it's one faced by many who have set up their own businesses. To be fair the dilemma is also experienced by many freelances and sole traders who find they have little or no time to work on the project that's close to their hearts. I do not think there are any simple solutions to this problem and can only suggest some approaches which may help you to think clearly.

- *Focus clearly from the outset.* I am not convinced that the demands of corporate work sit well with an ambition to make broadcast programmes or to develop long-term, larger-scale creative projects. In theory it should work well as a way of earning a living whilst developing a project. The trouble is that it doesn't always work out that way. If this question is a real one for you, then I think you have to spend some time in deciding what you priorities really are. It is essential that you answer some important questions very directly, completely honestly and as soon as you can.

    – Does the project really exist or is it simply a *nice* idea?

— Are you convinced that the project is viable both creatively and practically?

— What is the level of commitment you have to develop the project?

The answer to these questions should help you to focus clearly on your goals.

- *If your creative project is your over-riding goal.* It could be better to spend your time looking for development funding and seed money from the many organisations which will consider such applications. It may not be wise to try to combine this with corporate work. There are some companies which do this successfully, but not many. Sometimes the ones that do so are large enough to have specialised areas within them so that the stresses of combining two potentially conflicting goals are minimised. You will still need to earn a living, but you might be better to try full-time or part-time work outside the audio-visual industries where the demands on your creative energy could be fewer. The difficulty with combining *corporate* and *creative* is that corporate work does demand a high degree of creativity and mental energy. It can also be physically demanding. The result is that there may not be much left over for any other creative activity like writing a film script.

- *If your creative project is not your over-riding goal.* In this case your priority is your business and your business clients and you clearly acknowledge that other plans may have to wait or be squeezed into relatively small amounts of time.

- *Teamwork can help.* If you do decide to try to combine corporate business with other projects, working as a group could help. It may help to keep up morale and to keep a clear focus on longer-term goals (the development of your project) as well as on short-term ones (looking after your clients).

- *Plan ahead.* Even the most creative ventures need careful planning. Time should be set aside according to an agreed scheme to take the development forward and to avoid missing important deadlines for submitting ideas to funding bodies. Research into such practical aspects will be just as important as exercising your collective imagination.

9
Issues and ethics

From broken contracts and poor working conditions to lack of career progression and age discrimination, freelances suffer some of the worst experiences TV has to offer . . .
Edinburgh International Television Festival Programme 2003

In the middle of the 2003 Edinburgh International Television Festival, an event took place entitled *Freelance Hell.* The forum was part of the programme aimed specifically at young people aspiring to work in television. It was billed rather chillingly in the following terms:

> we'll be asking why freelance misery has become endemic, and grilling Execs from broadcasters and production companies to find the causes, effects and possible solutions.[39]

It will, therefore, come as no surprise to discover that there are a number of important issues and ethical concerns which are of particular concern to the freelance, although to some degree they affect the industry as a whole. Many of them are to do with your own well-being, happiness and success in your chosen field, others are more focused on those around you; the subjects of your programmes, your employers and your audiences. I have already pointed out the very high degree of motivation that is needed by anyone seeking to enter the audio-visual industry in any capacity, and that, in most cases, this motivation together with basic skills and a willingness to learn will (eventually) pay off. I have talked to many freelances in the course of preparing this book and it was arresting to observe that not one of those I spoke to said that they wanted to be a freelance! Without exception, all of them would have preferred a staff job. I can make no claims whatever for the representative accuracy of my sample, but my experience does seem to have at least some significance. A tracking survey of the industry carried out by the British Film Institute (BFI) and published in 1999 discovered that, of its sample

> the majority (56%) of respondents indicated that they would prefer to be working as staff. 29% indicated a preference for freelance work and 10%

*indicated a preference for work outside TV altogether. Those in post
production and technical roles were those most likely to state a preference
for freelance work.*[40]

It may well be that some of the issues we are about to explore are at the root of
some of the reservations about life as a freelance. I should quickly point out that
most of those with whom I have spoken considered themselves very happy and, in
many ways, privileged to do the work they were doing – it's just that they would
prefer to be doing it in a permanent job. Employment data suggest however that
the so-called casualisation of the industry is a trend that is likely to continue in
the foreseeable future.

FREELANCES UNDER PRESSURE

Isolation – I have a friend who has spent all his life as a successful trade union official intervening on behalf of others and trying to the best of his ability to secure
the best possible terms and conditions for his members, often in difficult and
trying circumstances. Now in retirement he frequently advises others on a more
informal basis on how to secure their rights. I've often been struck by how
assertive he requires other people to be, instructing them (the employee) to 'just
tell them' (the employer), 'that you're just not going to do it!' or whatever firm
approach is needed to head off the wayward employer. Of course for most of us it
is quite easy to stick up for someone else, but far more difficult to do it for our-
selves. This dilemma lies at the heart of what it is to be a freelance; basically,
you're on your own and you have to fight your own battles if you feel you are
being treated unfairly. Moving from project to project makes it difficult to establish and sustain supportive relationships. Statistical information for the industry
tells us that the proportion of the workforce on freelance contracts is highest for
the youngest age groups. Whilst being young may enable workers to be resilient
and energetic, youth and inexperience may also produce stress, loneliness, isolation and, most importantly, vulnerability.

Financial pressure – it would be a mistake to assume that stress is restricted to the
early days of freelance youth and inexperience. Family and financial pressures may
well increase as your career develops. Periods of unemployment or work shortage
assume a far greater significance when a family home is at risk if the mortgage is
not paid. In the journalism field, the National Union of Journalists (NUJ) has
expressed its concerns and has undertaken a research project to investigate a range
of problems which affect freelance well-being.

Work/life balance – whilst this is perhaps an inelegant phrase, it expresses an
important factor in maintaining mental and emotional well-being. There are pressures to perform and achieve which may be related to financial security but are
quite distinct from it. Part of the way in which freelances market themselves is to

appear successful and fulfilled whether they are feeling such confidence or not. They are aware of the old phrase *you're only as good as your last job* and this can put an enormous strain on an individual. There is the pressure to work over long hours. This can not only endanger health by overtiredness and sheer exhaustion, but has serious health and safety implications. Tired individuals are far more likely to have accidents both on set or location, but, perhaps more seriously, in driving between jobs or from home to work. The fact that freelances have to travel sometimes great distances increases the risk of car accidents and therefore serious injury and death. I am not aware of any specific research into this area, but actuarial evidence could be the reason for the very high premiums for car insurance generally offered to anyone working in the industry.

Working from home – means taking your work home and being available at all times; it means responding to the insistent ringing of the telephone just because the call might be bringing the next job. Most freelance jobs in the media industries demand a committed response and may well require considerable physical, creative and emotional contributions from the individual. If this is combined with a situation where there is no respite and the home does not provide a haven with some kind of protection from the demands of work, the resulting stress may become significant and have a negative impact on emotional well-being as well as on relationships and family interaction.

ARE THERE ANY SOLUTIONS?

It would be depressing and probably irresponsible to point out so many negative aspects of working as a freelance in the media industries and as a freelance without considering some possible solutions. Many of the stress-inducing situations encountered by the freelance are identical to those facing anyone in a similar role in the industry. What distinguishes the freelance from the employee in such situations is that the freelance is effectively alone. Additionally, whilst for the sake of convenience and clarity I have isolated and itemised some of the difficulties the freelance is likely to encounter, such stresses and strains are unlikely to make their presence felt one at a time! They are more likely to be experienced as a complex web of interrelated issues which may as a result seem even more insoluble. So what can you do? In many ways the act of defining and analysing the problems and the sources of stress may contain the key to eliminating them or at least coming to terms with them.

Isolation – the most constructive way to combat the isolation of working as a freelance is to begin to construct your own support networks. Informal arrangements can be built up, so that as a sound recordist, for example, you may become the preferred co-worker, generally recommended by a camera man or camera woman. Such arrangements are not going to fall into place instantly; it will take time for relationships of trust to develop. Equally, it will be unrealistic to expect to be part of a regular crew all the time; production companies will want to give work on a *horses for courses* basis. In other words, producers and directors will seek to give work to the most suitable person for the project in hand. There may be others that have specialisms that make them more suitable for a particular project. A constructive start would be to identify those with whom you would at least like to work on a regular basis and at the appropriate moment to sound them out as to their reaction. It may help to be on the books of an agency specialising in the provision of crews to production companies and broadcasters. This too is likely to lead to a pattern of working with other crew members on a regular, if not exclusive, basis. Fortunately there are some ready-made support networks available to the freelance and generally these will address a variety of issues of concern to the freelance. This chapter began with a reference to the Edinburgh TV festival session, *Freelance Hell*. Partly in response to some of the problems and abuses that emerged, Skillset in Scotland in association with other industry groups initiated a series of gatherings under the banner *Freelance Haven*. The emphasis is on informal learning and networking opportunities. This example from Scotland will be replicated in other areas across the UK and it will not be difficult to discover opportunities in your own geographical location. Contact information can be found in the reference section of this book. In addition to organisations like Skillset, other professional bodies do a great deal to foster relationships within the media industries. Organisations like The Royal Television Society (RTS) and BAFTA may well have regular meetings in your area. Inevitably the question of membership fees will arise but you may well consider that the money is well spent if it provides a valuable source of contacts, support and industry information and networking opportunities. Trade unions can play a vital role in this respect too. In addition to the support they are able to provide in social and networking opportunities, their expertise in matters of law, health and safety, and information about the *going rate for the job* is invaluable. There is, of course, a limit on the amount a freelance (and especially a new freelance) will wish to spend on trade union or professional association fees. I think however that it is worth putting membership near the top of your list of priorities. As a ready-made source of professional, legal, social and professional networks, membership will usually be very good value for money. A comprehensive list of relevant industry, professional and trade union bodies is provided in Chapter 10.

Finance – if financial insecurity is a persistent anxiety, then taking some steps, however modest, to begin to plan for the future may alleviate stress. It is important to begin to plan for the short, medium and long term. You should not jump to conclusions about what is and what is not possible for you as a freelance in financial matters. Investing in a home may well be possible despite irregular earnings and lean patches so the best advice is to consult an expert to find out what is possible in your particular circumstances. Chapter 8 gives some more detailed information on how to seek appropriate financial advice.

PRODUCTIONS UNDER PRESSURE

From time to time, productions, often of a factual or documentary nature, come under severe pressure because of their content. BBC television settled a dispute with the Elite model agency in 2001 concerning allegations of sexual impropriety contained in a *MacIntyre Undercover* programme aired in 1999. The BBC conceded that its portrayal of the agency was unfair. However, the same reporter went on to win libel damages against Kent police over allegations the force made about his undercover reporting methods. Initial controversy and criticism surrounded *The Secret Policeman* and reporter Mark Daly's exposé of racism within the Greater Manchester Police Force. Such misgivings quickly dissolved once the programme had been screened, and Home Secretary David Blunkett withdrew his original criticism of the programme as a 'covert stunt' and conceded that it had raised significant issues. Such programmes regularly explore the boundaries of accepted practice in programme making and often justify their approach on the grounds of public interest and the need to inform the audience of serious wrongdoing which would otherwise go undetected.

There is evidence, however, of increasing disquiet and anxiety about programme making practices in factual entertainment programmes which have little or no serious claim to expose anything of vital concern to the public interest. *Broadcast* magazine carried an opinion piece about a European conference of producers engaged in reality TV programming that took place in 2003. The most significant topic of conversation and discussion focused on a

> desire to frame a policy for the company that enshrined the notion of ethical behaviour.[41]

The article recognised that some decisions in broadcasting are easy to call; votes should not be rigged in shows that poll viewers, reconstructions in documentaries should be clearly signalled and not passed off as actuality, and prizes should actually be awarded. Other decisions, however, were less clear-cut:

> how many of us have coaxed members of the public to appear on television even though we know that sometimes that one appearance can change their life forever? It is easy enough to fall back on the defence of 'they knew what they were doing' but as we all know, most people have no idea how much they can expose themselves.[42]

This evidence of a growing degree of disquiet is all the more significant because it appears to have arisen from within the industry and not as a direct result of criticism from audiences or regulators. There are, however, significant professional pressures increasingly experienced throughout the industry to which the freelance worker is particularly vulnerable. This is not to say that the freelance is more likely then anyone else to make questionable decisions when under pressure, but it is only realistic to recognise that such pressure will weigh even more heavily on those who have the most to lose should they fail to do what is expected of them.

Two areas are of particular importance: that of participation and that of the way the story is treated.

Participation and informed consent

Factual programmes cannot be made unless people take part in them. This participation may be of a relatively innocuous nature; for example, a home may be used as the basis of a makeover programme and members of the family will no doubt appear as part of the programme. In other programme strands, however, the participation is of a more personal and intimate nature and may reveal a great deal about those taking part. In agreeing to take part, members of the public give their consent to the broadcasting of material in which they appear. The crucial ethical question is whether such consent is fully informed. Do the participants understand just how revealing their appearance might be, not simply by what is said or in answer to questions, but by body language, expression and unspoken behaviour, not to speak of the editing of the recorded material? The degree to which a producer has a responsibility to protect an adult from the consequences of their own actions (i.e. taking part in the programme) is not an easy one to judge. Clearly the producer has a much clearer understanding of the process and its consequences than the contributor. On the other hand, it is more than likely that the contributor has watched a great deal of television including the kind of programme they have been invited to take part in. Yet it is interesting to note how genuinely ignorant members of the public can be about the consequences of their *fifteen minutes of fame* and how unprepared they can be for sudden celebrity or notoriety.

Producers often make special provision for counselling and psychological help when such problems can be easily anticipated, though there must be many situations in which such help is neither anticipated nor provided. Even the provision of such support tends to overlook the issue of the scope of informed consent.

The principal focus is, of course, on the participant and often ignores the friends, family and others who may inadvertently be sucked into the consequent publicity. An upstanding member of the community who consents to take part in a docusoap, for example, may have no skeletons to keep hidden in the closet. They may, however, have overlooked, or be completely ignorant of facts about friends or family members which these individuals would much rather have continued to conceal.

The responsibility of the producer or broadcaster is, of course, to behave ethically in all dealings with members of the public. However, it is unlikely that the producer could be held to be responsible for the treatment the press may give to those who participate in factual entertainment or for unsavoury revelations about those who are not central to the programme but peripherally involved with it.

Treatment of story

The growth of factual entertainment has led to programmes where there is great pressure on producers to convey drama and conflict and to portray closure and resolution in order to satisfy the natural desire of the audience to know the outcome. Formulas and templates for these kinds of programmes often dictate exactly where in each episode problems, tensions and disagreements need to occur in order to keep audience attention at its peak. Hollywood writers are, of course, used to the pressures applied by the studio system for drama scripts to come up with these key twists and conflicts at particular moments. As writers of fiction, they are free to do so, and in this sense are not constrained by ethical considerations when they manipulate either their stories or their protagonists.

Ethical issues arise, however, when these programme requirements are imposed on the lives of ordinary people who take part in factual programming. As we have seen, whether they have been coaxed or have rushed to claim their fifteen minutes of fame, such individuals are highly vulnerable to the unfortunate consequences of the exposure such appearances may entail. These consequences may well be exacerbated by the subtle (or less subtle) manipulation of the story to provide the conflict and drama required by the audience and the commissioner. The producer or director may be tempted to apply pressure to coax or manipulate the subject of the programme to behave in a certain way or to undertake particular courses of action to satisfy the needs of the programme format. In turn, the producer is also under pressure to supply the drama and conflict, tension and resolution to fulfil the requirements of the commissioner who needs to justify his budget spend by the ratings his programmes achieve.

These ethical dilemmas form part of the decision-making undertaken by many producers on an almost daily basis. This is not a book about broadcasting ethics, yet in many ways, freelances, who *are* the subject of this book, might be seen as particularly vulnerable to pressures to manipulate their contributors or their contributors' stories to a greater degree than they would wish. The suggestion that these pressures may be largely self-imposed because of the particular vulnerabilities and insecurities of the freelance status only serves to underline the importance of a strong personal ethic and a high degree of integrity when it comes to resisting them.

EQUALITY OF OPPORTUNITY

Equality of opportunity is the right of every individual and that right has been enacted by Parliament. The opposite of equality of opportunity is discrimination, and this is proscribed in various pieces of legislation. It is very important to understand at the outset that your rights in this respect are guaranteed by the law. This does not of course ensure that every individual will enjoy the benefit of such legislation without fighting for it. In order to claim your rights, you need to understand them. This is an appropriate moment to consider a number of issues related to equality of opportunity in the media industries. Four main pieces of legislation safeguard your rights:

- Equal Pay Act 1970;

- Sex Discrimination Act 1975;

- Race Relations Act 1976;

- Disability Discrimination Act 1995.

In addition, amendments have also been enacted to widen the scope and to update this legislation. More recently, regulations to bring the UK into line with European directives have been enacted covering the areas of sexual orientation and religious beliefs.

Freelance perspective

It is very unclear at the moment what protection freelances can expect under various pieces of legislation concerning equality and discrimination. Obviously this is a matter for the lawyers and employment specialists. It is a major step for an employee to take action against an employer if he or she feels that treatment has been unfair. The situation of a freelance who feels the victim of discrimination or unfair treatment is complex and difficult. The degree of protection (if any) will depend on how the law regards the employment status of the freelance. At present, protection is given to *employees* and sometimes extends to *workers* (see Chapter 1). The scope of such coverage does change, however, as the government implements measures required by European directives. Nothing in this chapter or in this book should be taken as a statement of the law but only as a general guide to legislation current at the time of writing. As in all such matters, anyone who feels that they have been treated unfairly should seek advice and help as soon as possible, either from a competent trade union official or from a lawyer.

Gender

The latest available Skillset census results (for 2003) indicate that the proportion of women involved in the audio-visual industry remains relatively stable at around two-fifths of the total workforce and figures suggest that women account for between one-third and two-fifths of the freelance workforce.[43] It should, of course, be remembered that, traditionally, women have accounted for a larger proportion (over 75 per cent) of the workforce in some sectors like costume and wardrobe and make-up and hairdressing. The Skillset report points out that there appears to be a trend of increasing representation of women in key, high-end occupational groups like camera, sound and lighting. Here again we are talking about the industry as a whole, and not specifically freelance workers. It is also worth bearing in mind that the representation of women in the sectors just mentioned is very low. Women in camera, for example, appear to have increased their representation from 10 per cent to 18 per cent of the total workforce in the sector.

The Sex Discrimination Act (1975) clearly 'prohibits sex discrimination against individuals in the areas of employment, education and the provision of goods, facilities and services and in the disposal and management of premises'.[44] Sex discrimination may be direct, when a woman or a man is treated less favourably than a person of the opposite sex in comparable circumstances. Indirect discrimination occurs 'where a condition or practice is applied to both sexes, but adversely affects a considerably larger proportion of one sex than another'.[45] The protection offered to the freelance is slightly unclear, although the Act:

> *also protects people who are not employees in the sense required for some other employment rights, such as the right not to be unfairly dismissed.* It protects people engaged under a contract personally to execute work or labour. *Contract workers whose labour is supplied by their employer to another person (the principal) are protected against discrimination by the principal* . . .
>
> Equal Opportunities Commission Website (my emphasis)

This would certainly suggest that some freelances would be covered by the protection this legislation provides.

The Equal Pay Act (1970) – is the relevant legislation which gives the individual the right to the same pay and benefits as a person of the opposite sex engaged in comparable or equivalent work. The scope of the act is similar to that relating to sex discrimination (see above) in that it covers not only employees in the narrow legal sense, but also to 'other people who are engaged under a contract personally to execute work or labour'.[46] Sex discrimination and equal pay fall under the responsibility of the Equal Opportunities Commission. The website gives a great deal of useful information including advice on what steps to take if you think you've been the victim of discrimination in this area. Full contact information is available in the reference section in Chapter 10.

Race

Most of the available data suggest that representation of ethnic minorities might be a bright spot in the employment pattern of the audio-visual industries. They appear to form a rather higher proportion of the workforce in the industry than in the UK workforce as a whole. Data from 2002 indicates that 7.3 per cent of free-lances were of ethnic minority origin. In the industry as a whole, however, figures from 2003 indicate a decrease in representation from 8.2 per cent to 7.4 per cent. There is some suggestion, however, that these changes might be as a result of some changes in the scope and coverage of the census.[47] Broadcast television and the independent production sectors have shown a clear year-on-year increase in the representation of ethnic minorities.

The Race Relations Act (1976 and subsequent amendments) – according to the Commission for Racial Equality, the act 'makes it an offence to treat a person less favourably than others on racial grounds. These cover grounds of race, colour, nationality (including citizenship), and national or ethnic origin'.[48] Like discrimination on the grounds of sex, racial discrimination may be both direct and indirect. Discrimination is direct when a person is treated less favourably on racial grounds. Discrimination is indirect when, on grounds of colour or nationality, an individual is less likely to be able to comply with a requirement or condition and that requirement cannot be justified on non-racial grounds. Legislation in 2003 enlarged the scope of indirect discrimination to include a situation when 'a provision, criterion or practice is applied to everyone, but puts people of the same race or national or ethnic origin at a particular disadvantage'.[49] In all these circumstances, if you feel you have been discriminated against on racial grounds such as these, you will have to demonstrate that you have suffered disadvantage as a result. The Commission for Racial Equality has the particular responsibility to tackle racial discrimination and promote racial equality. Complaints on the grounds of racial discrimination are taken before employment tribunals or county courts (sheriff courts in Scotland). The CRE website has a great deal of information and full contact information is provided in Chapter 10.

Disability

The representation of disabled employees is reported by employers in the audio-visual industries as just below 1 per cent with a similar figure (1 per cent) for free-lance workers. Interestingly, 3 per cent of the workforce questioned reported having a disability, though possibly this discrepancy might be explained by differences in the methodology between the two surveys. However, on the surface it looks as if people with disabilities are significantly under-represented in the media industries. The Disability Rights Commission (DRC) estimates that about 13 per cent of the current UK workforce are disabled. Compare that with an apparent maximum 3 per cent for the audio-visual industries and the under-representation seems to be quite serious. Such conclusions need to be treated carefully, however, because the age profile of workers in the audio-visual industries is significantly lower than that of the workforce as a whole and research suggests a correlation between disability and age.[50] Nevertheless, from the available evidence it would probably be fair to conclude that broadcasting has not been particularly disability friendly as an occupation.

The Disability Discrimination Act 1995 (and subsequent amendments) – this is a very wide ranging piece of legislation covering many aspects of life and activity, such as access to buildings, education and social welfare provision. Most importantly in this present context, however, it covers employment whether that is full-time, part-time, apprenticeship or contract. The law specifically relates to employers with fifteen or more employees. The most important thing about the legislation, however, is that it makes it unlawful for an employer to discriminate against you if you are disabled, and this applies to the process of selection as well as the terms and conditions you may be offered. Promotion, benefits, dismissal and redundancy are also key areas covered by the law. If a dispute arises between an employer and a worker then a complaint can be made to the employment tribunal. The Disability Rights Commission is the independent body established in April 2000 by Act of Parliament to stop discrimination and promote equality of opportunity for disabled people.[51]

Industry perspective – not surprisingly employers and other organisations within the audio-visual industry have been taking disability issues seriously and have formed the Broadcasting and Creative Industries Disability Network (BCIDN). Most Broadcasters are members of the network, along with the independent producers group PACT and Skillset. The aim of the group in its own words is *to explore and address disability as it relates to the media industry*. The recruitment and retention of disabled people within the industry are key interests, as well as sharing best practice. Members of the network have undertaken to produce disability action plans, and these cover not only employment issues within member organisations but address the representation of disabled people on air, both on radio and television. The BCIDN have collaborated to produce a guide to disability issues, *Adjusting the Picture*, for those working in the industry, and this is available from the Employers' Forum on Disability.

Sexuality and religious belief

At the end of 2003 two pieces of legislation came into effect, effectively bringing the UK into line with European law. These statutory instruments extended the protection afforded to employees, and outlawed discrimination on the grounds of sexual orientation and religious belief.

The Employment Equality (Sexual Orientation) Regulations 2003 made it an offence to discriminate in employment on the grounds of sexual orientation. The new law covers recruitment, terms and conditions, benefits and other employment issues. Again, the concepts of direct and indirect discrimination apply, so that it becomes illegal to treat someone less favourably on the grounds of their sexual orientation (direct discrimination) or to impose requirements, conditions or practices which cause a disadvantage to someone because of their sexual orientation.

The Employment Equality (Religion or Belief) Regulations 2003 made it an offence to discriminate in terms of recruitment, employment, terms and conditions and so forth on the grounds of religious belief. Once again the concepts of direct and indirect discrimination apply in exactly the same way as for sexual orientation.

As for other areas of dispute, when an employer and employee fail to agree, the employee has recourse to the industrial tribunal.

AGE

More than 40 per cent of the adult population is aged fifty and over. Although discrimination on the grounds of age (or ageism as it is often known) is not specifically illegal, the government has committed itself to implementing age-related legislation by 2006. A code of practice on age diversity has been published and employers have been encouraged to adopt non-ageist policies in all areas of recruitment, selection, training, promotion, redundancy and retirement. In addition, the government has initiated a campaign through the Department for Work and Pensions. *Age Positive* is a group within the department aiming to develop strategy and policies to support people making decisions about working and retirement.[52]

Industry perspective

It has been generally assumed that freelancing is a fruitful prospect for the over-fifties in the audio-visual industries. This group of workers clearly represents a huge pool of experience and expertise which should make them invaluable to any potential employer. For the freelance, or the potential freelance, the advantages seem to be fairly obvious; such work can provide both the freedom to choose projects and a way of managing working patterns as retirement approaches. Such an approach to 'flexible working' as it has become known has received considerable support from various groups and government working parties as well as in a number of publications. Recent research, however, has revealed a not-entirely positive situation and raises serious questions about freelancing for older people.[53] This research covered a wide range of individuals, including managers, individual freelancers and industry experts in a wide range of occupational activities in the media including journalism and broadcasting. There was some support for the benefits of flexibility that freelance work can offer the older worker in terms of choice, freedom and the lack of enforced retirement. The prevailing experience was, however, far less positive:

> Accounts of freelancing among older, as well as younger, people revealed this to be a relentless, precarious and often unsatisfying form of work. There were many stories of exploitation, mismanagement and unfair treatment. Rarely did they receive in-house training or financial help in meeting the costs of skills updates. Yet they were expected to offer optimum productivity during assignments, and to maintain high levels of energy, enthusiasm, commitment, reliability and competence.[54]

This reveals a down-side to freelancing which, coupled with the experiences recounted in *Freelance Hell*, discussed earlier in this chapter, has serious implications which should be carefully considered by anyone, of whatever age, contemplating a freelance career in the media industries.

NATIONS AND REGIONS

It is perhaps fitting that the geographical locus of freelance employment should be discussed at this point, and as part of a treatment of issues of diversity and equality of opportunity. It does seem that the relentless centrifugal force of London and the South East means that it may be difficult to sustain, or at least to develop, a freelance career in what are known in the broadcasting business as the *Nations and Regions*. Census information from Skillset suggests that the workforce of the audiovisual industry numbered around 140,000 in total in 2003, excluding those in the cinema exhibition sector. The vast bulk of workers, just over 75,000, or more than half the workforce, was working in London and the South East of England.[55] This metropolitan dominance seems to be even more pronounced in the freelance workforce where 65.5 per cent were working in London or the South East on census day. There has been a slight movement towards decentralisation since 1993.[56] Scotland and Wales are home to 7 per cent and 4 per cent of freelances respectively, whilst the figures for the East of England, 7 per cent, and the North West, 8 per cent, show significant numbers of freelances working in the industry. The pattern therefore seems to be for small but strong and relatively stable centres of freelance employment within the Nations and Regions, but for the overwhelming bulk of work to be concentrated in London and the South East. The immediate response might therefore be to assume that, in order to start and sustain a freelance career, it might be advisable to be based in the metropolitan area. It is worth considering a range of factors before coming to any conclusions. First, some of the advantages. London is the centre of broadcasting for the UK, and thus:

- it provides a wide range of opportunities in many industry sectors;

- opportunities are concentrated in a relatively small area;

- networking is consequently easier;

- communication may be better;

- there is a wide range of employers;

- training opportunities may be better;

- a wider variety of professional experience may be available to the individual worker;

- it provides a closer relationship to the hub of the industry.

On the other hand, working in the Nations and Regions may offer some compelling advantages too:

- a more manageable local audio-visual industry where it is easier to know the key players;

- the ability to gain experience in local or regional programming;

- a less pressurised lifestyle, shorter commutes and lower housing prices, for example;

- the possibility of less formal and therefore more flexible relationships within the industry;

- the possibility that those with considerable experience and expertise will rise more quickly to the top of the professional scale because they are more 'visible'.

Much of your choice will inevitably be based on personal preferences and on the kind of ambition that you harbour as an individual. There are those who prefer to be at what they perceive as the centre of the broadcasting world, whilst others are happiest in smaller, more identifiable communities. These should not be seen as issues of merit, status or prestige, but as genuine and important choices and preferences. They may well have a lasting impact not only on your professional satisfaction, but on how much you enjoy life in general. Change can be difficult for anyone to manage successfully, but it is also worth remembering that one of the advantages of the freelance life is that decisions do not have to be forever. It is possible for the freelance worker to change location (and lifestyle) rather more easily than for the employee to do so.

10
References and information

1 WHAT IS A FREELANCE?

Department for Work and Pensions
Correspondence Unit Room
540 The Adelphi, 1–11 John Adam Street, London WC2N 6HT
Tel.: 020 7712 2171
Fax: 020 7712 2386
Web: www.dwp.gov.uk

Inland Revenue List of Accepted Self Employed Grades
From time to time the Inland Revenue issues a list of occupations within all sectors of the film industry and to television broadcasting. This list, called *Film and Television Industry Guidance Notes*, is available from the Inland Revenue and from the trade union BECTU
Local enquiry helplines are available, you should consult your directory.
Documents can be downloaded from:
www.inlandrevenue.gov.uk

2 STARTING A FREELANCE CAREER

AGCAS (Association of Graduate Careers Advisory Services)
AGCAS Administration Office
Millennium House, 30 Junction Road, Sheffield S11 8XB
Tel.: 0114 251 5750
Fax: 0114 251 5751
Web: www.agcas.org.uk

Cyfle The National Training Provider for Television, Film and Interactive Media Industry in Wales
3rd Floor, Crichton House, 11–12 Mount Stewart Square, Cardiff CF10 5EE
Tel.: 029 2046 5533
Web: www.cyfle.co.uk

FT2 – training provider

For young people who wish to become freelance assistants in the construction, production and technical areas of the United Kingdom's film and television industry.
Web: www.ft2.org.uk

FT2 Film & Television Freelance Training

4th Floor, Warwick House, 9 Warwick Street, London W1B 5LY
Tel.: 020 7734 5141
Web: www.ft2.org.uk

Scottish Screen

Second Floor, 249 West George Street, Glasgow G2 4QE
Tel.: 0141 302 1700
Web: www.scottishscreen.com

Skillset – The Sector Skills Council for the Audio Visual Industries

Prospect House, 80–110 New Oxford Street, London WC1A 1HB
Tel.: +44 (0) 20 7520 5757
Fax: +44 (0) 20 7520 5758
Email enquiries: info@skillset.org
Web: www.skillset.org

UK TV Freelancers

A useful website which compiles information likely to be of use to freelances. Includes data on rates of payment, employers and holiday entitlement.
Web: www.tvfreelancers.org.uk

3 SUSTAINING AND DEVELOPING A FREELANCE CAREER

Skillset Career Helpline for England

Tel.: 08080 300 900

Skillset Career Helpline for Scotland

Tel.: 0808 100 8094

BFI/Skillset database of media and multimedia courses in the UK

Web: www.bfi.org.uk/education/courses/mediacourses/

National Union of Journalists (NUJ)
Head Office
Headland House, 308–312 Gray's Inn Road, London WC1X 8DP
Tel.: 020 7278 7916
Fax: 020 7837 8143
Email: info@nuj.org.uk
Web: www.nuj.org.uk

Broadcasting Entertainment Cinematograph and Theatre Union (BECTU)
Head Office
373–377 Clapham Road, London SW9 9BT
Tel.: 020 7346 0900
Fax: 020 7346 0901
Email: info@bectu.org.uk
Web: www.bectu.org.uk

BKSTS The Moving Image Society
Pinewood Studios, Iver Heath, Bucks SL0 0NH
Tel.: 01753 656656
Fax: 01753 657016
Web: www.bksts.com

Guild of Television Cameramen
General enquiries:
Tel.: 01822 614405
Web: www.gtc.org.uk/

Scottish Screen
Second Floor, 249 West George Street, Glasgow G2 4QE
Tel.: 0141 302 1700
Web: www.scottishscreen.com

Sgrin – Media Agency for Wales
The Bank, 10 Mount Stuart Square, Cardiff Bay, Cardiff CF10 5EE
Tel.: 02920 333300
Web: www.sgrin.co.uk

Northern Ireland Film and Television Commission
Alfred House, 21 Alfred Street, Belfast BT2 8ED
Tel.: 0289023 2444
Web: www.nifc.co.uk

UK Film Council
10 Little Portland Street, London W1W 7JG
Tel.: 020 77861 7861
Web: www.ukfilmcouncil.org.uk

Association of Graduate Careers Advisory Service (AGCAS)
Web: www.agcas.org.uk

The association responsible for the **Prospects website**, an invaluable resource for employment, training and education advice (see AGAS above)
Web: www.prospects.ac.uk

4 FREELANCING IN RADIO

BBC – Employment in Engineering
BBC Recruitment
PO Box 48305, London, W12 6YE
Tel.: 0870 333 1330
Textphone: 020 8008 4300
Email: recruitment@bbc.co.uk
Web: www.bbc.co.uk/jobs

Manx Radio – Engineering
A helpful insight into radio engineering outside London
Manx Radio Ltd
PO Box 1368, Douglas, Isle of Man IM99 1SW
Tel.: 01624 682 600
Fax: 01624 682 604
Web: www.manxradio.com/engineering

Radio Academy
5 Market Place, London, W1W 8AE
Tel.: 020 7255 2010
Fax: 020 7255 2029
Email: info@radioacademy.org
Web: www.radioacademy.org

Student Radio Association
Web: www.studentradio.org.uk

Media UK – Industry Information and Directory

This is a very useful website full of news and industry chat. A very good way of keeping in touch with what's happening and for finding out about some of the jobs.

Web: www.mediauk.com

Broadcast Journalism Training Council (BJTC)

This body is responsible for the accreditation of eighteen college and university journalism training courses. The website provides industry training information and job details.

Web: www.bjtc.org.uk

Radio Magazine

Weekly industry magazine containing news information and jobs. Some of the content is available online. Contact, subscription and information is available from:

The Radio Magazine

Crown House, 25 High Street, Rothwell, Kettering NN14 6AD
Freepost Radio, or from the website
Web: www.theradiomagazine.co.uk

Hospital Broadcasting Association

The Hospital Broadcasting Association is a national charity which promotes and supports hospital broadcasting in the UK. The HBA represents over 250 member stations.

Web: www.hbauk.com

Global Radio News – An independent radio news supplier

292 Vauxhall Bridge Road, London SW1V 1AE
Tel.: 020 7976 5335
Fax: 020 7630 5461
Web: www.globalradionews.com

IRN – Independent Radio News

(Part of ITN)
Tel.: 020 7430 4090
Web: www.irn.co.uk

5 FREELANCING IN TELEVISION

British Academy of Film & Television Arts (BAFTA)
195 Piccadilly, London W1J 9LN
Tel.: 020 7734 0022
Fax: 020 7734 1792
Web: www.bafta.org

BBC Television
BBC TV Centre, Wood Lane, London W12 7RJ
Tel.: 020 8743 8000
Web: www.bbc.co.uk/

Channel 4 Television
124 Horseferry Road, London SW1P 2TX
Tel.: 020 77396 4444
Web: www.channel4.com

Five (Channel 5 Television)
22 Long Acre, London WC2E 9LY
Web: www.five.tv/

ITV
For programming information and access to the regional Channel 3 companies, look under Region
ITV Network Centre, 200 Gray's Inn Road, London WC1X 8HF
Tel.: 020 7843 8000
Fax: 020 7843 8158
Web: www.itv.com
For company information
ITV PLC
ITV PLC Head Office, The London Television Centre, Upper Ground, London SE1 9LT
Web: www.itvplc.com

Ofcom – The regulator for broadcasting and telecoms
Provides useful information about licences and codes and the radio and television industries in general.
Web: www.ofcom.gov.uk

Producers' Alliance for Cinema & Television (PACT)

PACT is a trade association for Independent Producers. The website has a great deal of information useful to freelances.

Pact

45 Mortimer Street, London W1W 8HJ

Tel.: 020 7331 6000

Fax: 020 7331 6700

Web: www.pact.co.uk/

Royal Television Society (RTS)

Industry Forum. Local meetings in most areas.

Holborn Hall, 100 Gray's Inn Road, London WC1X 8AL

Tel.: 020 7430 1000

Fax: 020 7430 0924

Web: www.rts.org.uk

S4C

Cardiff

Parc Ty Glas Llanishen, Cardiff CF14 5DU

Tel.: 029 20747444

Caernarfon

Lôn Ddewi, Caernarfon LL55 1ER

Tel.: 01286 674622

Web: www.S4C.co.uk

Sky – British Sky Broadcasting plc

For programming information and access to all Sky websites;

Web: www.sky.com

For corporate information:

British Sky Broadcasting Group

Grant Way, Isleworth TW7 5QD

Tel.: 020 7705 3000

If you want to look for contacts for particular channels on BSkyB, the best way is to use an Internet search engine. There is a very full directory listing of all these channels on Media UK.

Web: www.mediauk.com/directory/

6 FREELANCING IN NON-BROADCAST

International Visual Communication Association (IVCA)
IVCA Business Communication Centre, 19 Pepper Street, Glengall Bridge,
London E14 9RP
Tel.: 020 7512 0571
Web: www.ivca.org

7 PITCHING IDEAS

BBC Radio and Television provide extensive and detailed guidance on commissioning practice for industry professionals and members of the public.
Web: www.bbc.co.uk/commissioning/

ITV also has a plethora of useful information specifically aimed at producers.
Web: www2.itv.com/about/producers/

Channel 4 provides information on their website.
Web: www.channel4.com/4producers/

Five is not quite as easy to contact. The best advice is to log on to their website and follow the links 'about five' and look for the corporate pages.
Web: www.five.tv/

Research Centre for Television and Interactivity has undertaken a significant investigation into this whole area. *Inside the Commissioners* reveals a great deal of information about television commissioners and the commissioning process. This can be viewed online.
Web: www.researchcentre.co.uk

The Patent Office
Concept House, Cardiff Road, Newport, South Wales NP10 8QQ
Web: www.patent.gov.uk/

The UK Copyright Service
Web: www.copyrightservice.co.uk/

The Script Vault
Web: www.thescriptvault.com

Sources of funding
The film and television agencies listed in the section above (for Chapter 5) will have information about funding and may control certain funds themselves. In addition it is worth checking the following organisations:

UK MEDIA Desk
Fourth Floor, 66–68 Margaret Street, London W1W 8SR
Tel.: 020 7323 9733
Web: www.mediadesk.co.uk/england

MEDIA Antenna Wales
c/o SGRIN, 10 Mount Stuart Square, Cardiff Bay, Cardiff CF10 5EE
Tel.: 02920 333 304
Web: www.mediadesk.co.uk/wales

MEDIA Antenna Scotland
249 West George Street, Glasgow G2 4QE
Tel.: 0141 302 1776/7
Web: www.mediadesk.co.uk/scotland

MEDIA Services Northern Ireland
c/o Northern Ireland Film Commission
Third Floor, Alfred House, 21 Alfred Street, Belfast BT2 8ED
Tel.: 02890 232 444
Web: www.mediadesk.co.uk/northernireland

8 BUSINESS MATTERS

Business Link – Practical advice for business
A useful support and information network run by the Department for Trade and Industry. The website gives details of local operators in England.
Tel.: 0845 600 9 006
Web: www.businesslink.gov.uk

Business Eye in Wales
Tel.: 08457 96 97 98
Web: www.businesseye.org.uk

Business Gateway in Lowland Scotland
Tel.: 0845 609 6611
Web: www.bgateway.com

Highlands and Islands Enterprise
Tel.: 01463 244469
Web: www.hie.co.uk

Invest Northern Ireland
Tel.: 028 9023 9090
Web: www.investni.com

Financial Services Authority (FSA)
25 The North Colonnade, Canary Wharf, London E14 5HS
Tel.: 0845 606 1234
Web: www.fsa.gov.uk

HM Customs & Excise (for VAT matters)
Web: www.hmce.gov.uk

Inland Revenue
Runs a special help line service for new businesses and the newly self-employed
Tel.: 0845 915 4515; 08457 660 830 (in Welsh); 08459 153 296 (Mincom)

Starting Your Business
The Inland Revenue have produced an excellent hardcover guide free of charge which covers virtually everything you need to know. Unless you actually register a business it's only available as a download. If and when you register you can be sent a copy free of charge. To register as self-employed call the number above.
Web: www.ir.gov.uk/selfemployed/

Institute of Financial Planning
Whitefriars Centre, Lewins Mead, Bristol BS1 2NT
Tel.: 0117 945 2470
Fax: 0117 929 2214
Web: www.financialplanning.org.uk
enables you to search for advisers who are fee-based.

Prince's Scottish Youth Business Trust
6th Floor, 53 Bothwell Street, Glasgow G2 6TS
Tel.: 0141 248 4999
Web: www.psybt.org.uk
The Trust publishes a useful business start-up guide, available for download from the website. Loans and support are available.

Prince's Trust
The website contains information about Prince's Trust offices throughout the UK.
18 Park Square, East London NW1 4LH
Tel.: 020 7543 1234
Web: www.princes-trust.org.uk

Scottish Enterprise
5 Atlantic Quay, 150 Broomielaw, Glasgow G2 8LU
Tel.: 0141 248 2700
Web: www.scottish-enterprise.com

Society of Financial Advisers

The website allows you to search for advisers in your location who work on a fee or commission basis.
20 Aldermanbury Street, London EC2V 7HY
Tel.: 020 8989 8464
Web: www.sofa.org

9 ISSUES AND ETHICS

Employers' Forum on Disability

Nutmeg House, 60 Gainsford Street, London SE1 2NY
Tel.: 020 7403 3020
Fax: 020 7403 0404
Minicom: 020 7403 0050
Web: www.employers-forum.co.uk

Equal Opportunities Commission

Great Britain Office
Arndale House, Arndale Centre, Manchester M4 3EQ
Tel.: 0845 601 5901
Web: www.eoc.org.uk

Commission for Racial Equality

St Dunstan's House, 201–211 Borough High Street, London SE1 1GZ
Tel.: 020 7939 0000
Web: www.cre.gov.uk

Disability Rights Commission

DRC Helpline, FREEPOST MID02164, Stratford upon Avon CV37 9BR
Tel.: 08457 622 633
Textphone: 08457 622 644
Web: www.drc-gb.org

Age Positive

Age Positive Team, Department for Work and Pensions, Room W8d, Moorfoot, Sheffield S1 4PQ
Web: www.agepositive.gov.uk

Useful reading

Contracts of Employment – Employment Law Handbook (IDS) 2001.
Careers Handbook for TV, Radio, Film, Video and Interactive Media, Shiona Llewellyn and Sue Walker (A & C Black) 2003.
Guardian Media Directory, Emily Bell (ed.) (Atlantic Books) 2004.
The Insider Guide to Careers in Broadcasting and the Media, Karen Holmes (Spiro Press) 2000.
Radio Production – A Manual for Broadcasters, Robert McLeish (Focal Press) 1999.
Presenting on TV & Radio – An Insider's Guide, Janet Trewin (Focal Press) 2003.
Researching for Television and Radio, Adèle Emm (Routledge) 2001.
Multiskilling for Television Production, Peter Ward *et al*. (Focal Press) 2000.
Broadcast Journalism: Techniques of Radio and TV News, Andrew Boyd (Focal Press) 2000.
Lies, Damn Lies and Documentaries, Brian Winston (BFI) 2000.
Local Radio Journalism, Paul Chantler, Sim Harris (Focal Press) 1992.
Starting Your Own Business: How to Plan, Build and Manage, Jim Green (How to Books) 2002.
The 'Which?' Guide to Starting Your Own Business: How to Make a Success of Going It Alone, Which? (Which? Books) 2003.
The 'Daily Telegraph' Small Business Guide to Starting Your Own Business, Michael Becket (Pan) 2003.
The Television Handbook, Patricia Holland (Routledge) 2000.
The Radio Handbook, Carole Fleming (Routledge) 2002.

Notes

1 Rageh Omaar, quoted in the *Guardian Weekend*, 28 February 2004.
2 See, for example, information on both rates and employers at www.tvfreelancers. org.uk.
3 http://www.inlandrevenue.gov.uk.
4 http://www.bbc.co.uk/jobs/our_benefits/index.shtml.
5 Skillset Freelance Survey 2001 Executive Summary, p. 1.
6 Op. cit. and Skillset Workforce Survey 2003.
7 www.agcas.org.uk/index2.htm.
8 Morey *et al.* (2002) *Perceptions of the Media Studies Curriculum and Employability*, Birmingham, the Centre for Research into Quality.
9 For example, Ability Office (www.uk.ability.com) or Sun Star Office (www.sun.com/ staroffice). A search of online software reviews will usually bring up-to-date information on available suites.
10 http://jobs.guardian.co.uk/.
11 www.broadcastnow.co.uk.
12 www.filmbang.co.uk.
13 www.skillsformedia.com/resource/diary/index_1.asp.
14 Skillset, op. cit. 2002.
15 www.prospects.ac.uk.
16 http://www.ofcom.org.uk/about_ofcom/how_we_work/statutory_duties?a=87101.
17 www.ofcom.org.uk.
18 www.mediauk.com.
19 www.Ofcom.org.uk.
20 BJTC – Broadcast Journalism Training Council (www.bjtc.org).
21 www.hbauk.com.
22 www.studentradio.org.uk.
23 The Communications Act 2003.
24 Skillset Workforce Survey 2003.
25 Skillset Freelance Survey 2001 Appendix A.
26 Skillset website.
27 Preston, A. (2003) *Inside the Commissioners: The Culture and Practice of Commissioning at UK Broadcasters*, Glasgow, The Research Centre for Television and Interactivity.
28 The Alliance for the Protection of Copyright (APC) is an umbrella organisation comprising BECTU, the Writers' Guild, the Directors Guild, the NUJ, the Society of

Authors, Women in Film & Television, the MU, Radio Independents Organisation, the Scottish Independent Radio Producers Association and PACT.

29 TUC website, www.tuc.org.uk.
30 Quicken Software from Intuit, PO Box 4944, Twyford, Reading RG10 9BF, www.intuit.co.uk.
31 Microsoft Money, http://money.msn.co.uk.
32 Inland Revenue contact information: www.inlandrevenue.gov.uk/menus/contactus.shtml.
33 Financial Services Authority, 25 The North Colonnade, Canary Wharf, London E14 5HS, www.fsa.gov.uk/.
34 www.businesslink.gov.uk/. Business Link operates in England, and has affiliates in Scotland, Northern Ireland and Wales.
35 Contact details are available from: www.consumer.gov.uk/rda/info/.
36 Scottish Enterprise, 5 Atlantic Quay, 150 Broomielaw, Glasgow G2 8LU, www.scottish-enterprise.com.
37 Welsh Development Agency, Plas Glyndwr, Kingsway, Cardiff CF10 3AH, www.wda.co.uk/.
38 Invest Northern Ireland, 44–58 May Street, Belfast BT1 4NN, www.investni.com/.
39 Media Guardian Edinburgh International Television Festival – Programme 2003.
40 Television Industry Tracking Study – BFI Centre for Audience and Industry Research 1999, available for download at: www.bfi.org.uk/education/.
41 Goodwin, Daisy (2004) Doing the Right Thing, *Broadcast* 9 July.
42 Ibid.
43 Skillset census data 1999 (Freelance) and 2003 (General).
44 Equal Opportunities Commission, www.eoc.org.uk.
45 Ibid.
46 Ibid.
47 Skillset Census Data 2003, op. cit.
48 Commission for Racial Equality (CRE) website, www.cre.gov.uk.
49 Ibid.
50 Skillset Workforce Survey 2003, p. 24.
51 Disability Rights Commission (DRC), www.drc-gb.org.
52 www.agepositive.gov.uk.
53 Platman, A. (2002) *The Price of Freedom: The Myths and Realities of the Portfolio Career for Experienced, Older Professionals*, Milton Keynes, The Open University Business School.
54 Ibid. p. 9.
55 Skillset Census results 2003.
56 Skillset Freelance survey 2001.

Index